Exmoor's Maritime Heritage

Exmoor's
Maritime Heritage

JOHN GILMAN

EXMOOR
BOOKS

First published by Exmoor Books 1999

Copyright © John Gilman

ISBN 0 86183 480 1

Line drawings courtesy of Gordon Macfie

The views expressed by the author are his own and are not necessarily those of the Exmoor National Park Authority

British Library Cataloguing-in-publication Data

A CIP catalogue record for this book is available from the British Library.

EXMOOR BOOKS
Official Publisher to the Exmoor National Park Authority.

EXMOOR BOOKS
Dulverton, Somerset

Trade sales enquires:
Halsgrove
Halsgrove House
Lower Moor Way
Tiverton, EX16 6SS
Tel: 01884 243242
Fax: 01884 243325

Exmoor Books is a partnership between
The Exmoor Press and The Exmoor National Park

Printed and bound in Great Britain by WBC Ltd, Bridgend

CONTENTS

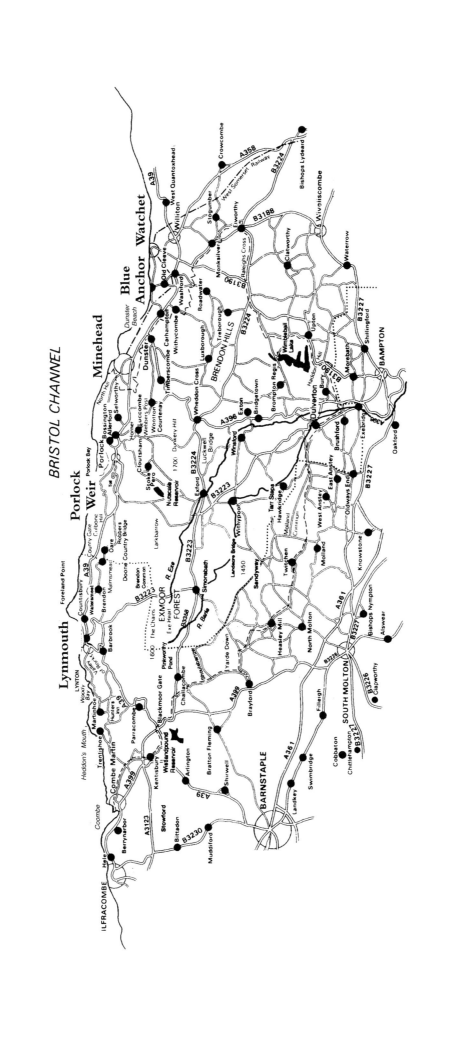

DEDICATION

One man, perhaps above all other, influenced my interest in the little seaports of West Somerset and North Devon. He was Captain Philip Stanley Rawle (Stan) 1895-1972, a regular voyager from Minehead and a marvellous man, long remembered for his lively humour and great strength of character. He holds a place in local history as the last master and owner of a vessel trading out of West Somerset and was harbour master at Minehead for many years. He had that rare wit and teasing sense of humour that was the mark of the old sailorman. Even this description does not really justify his depth, humour and generosity. Fifty years ago he encouraged me to discover the heart of West Somerset's small seaport towns and villages and by patient encouragement urged me to build a collection of memories still extant at that time. Just as he took me to sea with him and tolerated my clumsy attempts at seamanship, so he listened to my early literary efforts and remains, even now, my judge as to whether I have got my facts right. I dedicate this selection of pictures of the Exmoor ports to him and his family.

My grateful thanks are also extended to everyone who has assisted me over the years with photos, stories, myths, legends and ancient local gossip. When it came to selecting the material from a collection of fifty years and presenting some of the stories and folk lore of the region I owe a tremendous debt to Annie Jordan, whose patient help has enabled me to share this with you.

Perhaps more than anything else, this book illustrates just how much has changed over the last century, not only environmentally but socially and culturally. It is my hope that through this small collection I have been able to open a window into the past not only for local families who treasure their heritage but for the thousands of visitors who come to this part of Exmoor to enjoy its special magic.

John Gilman 1999

EXMOOR'S MARITIME HERITAGE

A Personal View

by John Gilman

The Exmoor harbours of North Devon and West Somerset have a fascinating and extended history. Lynmouth, Porlock Weir, Minehead, Dunster and Watchet are all long established ports which have grown, developed and decayed over the centuries from before the conquest. Each has had its high points and Minehead for example once enjoyed a position among the prominent ports of the United Kingdom with well established links to the West Indies and America with the largest ships of the day. Watchet, possibly the oldest of all, probably had its origins in the Mediterranean trade when Phoenician seafarers regularly visited this sheltered Bristol Channel creek port. Porlock Weir and Dunster, both over a thousand years old, are weir harbours and Dunster Haven saw the export of expedition equipment in support of Henry V in his French campaign. Lynmouth and Porlock remained relatively isolated for centuries and continued as domestic ports for the import of every necessary commodity until the advent and development of rail and road transport. Each port evolved a local fishing industry and each became unique in its approach to local conditions and developed a reputation for vessels, methods and skills. In the seventeenth century Minehead exported herrings nationwide occasioning the little rhyme

> *Herrings and bread*
> *Go the bells of Minehead*

whilst Porlock Weir oysters were prized in the restaurants and hotels of London.

Of all these little harbours, Porlock Weir remains quite unique. Firstly because it is a rare survival of one of Britain's earliest types of haven or harbour and secondly because it has hardly grown or shrunk for a thousand years. These early forms of weir harbour establish themselves in an existing land form, in this case a stream bed lying within a shingle bank and filled twice daily by a wide range of tides. We have in Porlock Weir a remarkable example of a harbour type that was once familiar on many shingle coasts but is now quite rare. Its age is also quite remarkable as weir havens formed in the small streambeds and creeks that ran inside shingle banks were common in Saxon times. Porlock Weir, Minehead and Dunster Hawn are certainly examples that owe their origin to this era of commercial coastal development. Because the entrance to Porlock Weir harbour was established in stone and mortar, probably early in the fifteenth century, it survived whilst Dunster Hawn's entrance was allowed to decay and fill up by natural drift and Minehead's has disappeared altogether.

To understand the idea of the weir harbour and how they were adapted and modified for commercial use it is useful to see how they developed and maintained themselves as bodies of water within the protection of a shingle bank. Even without a feeder stream and formed by natural springs and run-off from higher ground, they formed ponds that could last for centuries. With a feeder stream, they became potential harbours as the stream inevitably found its way to the sea and forced an entrance through the bank which could be widened, strengthened and made permanent. A wide range of tides on this coast was a significant contributory factor as daily the flow was reversed and the weir backed up until the tide's full height was achieved within the bank.

Luckily there are aerial photographs showing weir ponds and a photograph of Greenaleigh Pond in 1947 (below) shows just how a weir would look before development. Greenaleigh Pond's acreage has fluctuated over the centuries but from this photograph it is clear just how it was formed. With no outlet and no feeder stream this particular feature has remained untouched and will eventually decay through natural infill. By studying aerial photographs of this coast over fifty years it is possible to make informed and reliable guesses as to the sites of the weir harbours which formed the basis or nucleus of nautical settlement and early trade in the region. Of particular value was the RAF survey of 1947 which was undertaken in April after winter precipitation and ground saturation had left the old stream and contributory beds prominent. Dunster Hawn's extensive harbour shows clearly as does the large decayed weir below Carhampton which probably predated the Hawn and was the outlet for the considerable early Saxon set-

tlement at Carhampton where, incidentally, a large Saxon burial site has been confirmed. Immediately off the coast there still remains a complicated system of ridges and banks which would have been tricky to navigate and probably contributed to its eventual decline and the succession of the Hawn after the conquest under Norman administration.

Once established, the weir harbour could be deepened, widened and lined with mortared stone to provide wharves and quays to receive vessels. Contemporary evidence shows that ocean-going vessels of considerable size, and up to one hundred tons, used local weir harbours successfully for centuries and might continue to do so unless the entrance failed or the weir itself became silted up due to its parent stream altering course. It was for both reasons that the weir harbour at Minehead failed; the stream altered its course and the entrance, despite attempts to rectify the matter, became increasingly clogged with beach stones. In the case of the Bratton Water at Minehead the situation might have been reversed but at the time Minehead had just obtained a charter for self-determination and subsequently leased the harbour to private enterprise, the upkeep of which became too great to meet with the income from the duty payable by harbour traffic. The Luttrell family, Lords of the Manor, washed their hands of the matter as the harbour was no longer under their control and they commenced building a new projecting quay extending into deep water some four hundred metres to the westward rather than subsidise the town's faltering old weir and breakwater which, over the ensuing years, failed, was filled up and built over.

It might even have been before Saxon times that these little havens came into existence because they offered immediate shelter for vessels of up to forty feet in length on an otherwise iron-bound coast. So successful was this form of harbour that it often occasioned the development of early settlement. In the detailed analysis of local longshore drift, tides and the pattern of drainage into the Bristol Channel in this region over the last millennium, three significant sites emerge. The biggest was likely to have been where the River Avill crosses the alluvial flats beneath Conygar Hill to meet the shingle banks converging near Knaplock Point. At this point the river swung eastward before finding an exit through the shingle where the tides exerted maximum impact on the clay. This entrance would need constant work to keep clear and a channel for deep water cargo vessels would need to be kept clear at low tide and marked for safe passage. Although the name 'Weir' implies a sheltered harbour inlet earlier derivations echo the old Norse word *veor* which indicated a hidden or secret haven. It is probable but not certain that this type of harbour was used by Danish marauders on their sorties to the west of England. Today there still exists a vestige of Dunster's sea port and it is called The Hawn which is a corruption of haven. It was still in use in the fifteenth century although on the development of the port of Minehead where deep sea vessels could ride in safety the port of Dunster was allowed to decay.

As mentioned above, there was a weir harbour or haven at Minehead. Although not on as large a scale as that provided by the River Avill at Dunster, nevertheless it was sufficiently large for cargo vessels to lie sheltered within its walls. This was created by the Bratton Water meeting the shingle ridge at a point near the bottom of the present Avenue and deflecting northwest until it reached Quay Street. Similar to the pattern at Porlock Weir the entrance would have been protected from longshore drift by a projecting stone and timber framed jetty. Like Porlock Weir the entrance would have been tidal affording a good depth of water within the weir. It is highly likely that quays and buildings would have been constructed on both sides, probably as far upstream as The Red Lion which was the old focus of commercial harbour traffic. Luckily for the historian some evidence of this weir harbour still existed when a survey was done of the foreshore in 1701 and a note made that a pond was connected to the old 'peer'. The same survey gives the site of the old quay which developed from the jetty at the weir's mouth. That this was the old harbour head is further evidenced by the fact that the old lane to Higher Town linked to the shore here and in fact still exists to this day.

There is also evidence that this weir harbour was much decayed by the end of the fifteenth century with contemporary traffic depending on the quay at the entrance. The chief danger to a tidal reach no longer fed by its parent stream is that it can quickly fill up which is why in 1483 we read of a prohibition against throwing stones into the weir. Once the original stream had made its new entrance to the sea, probably due to storm damage, the whole system fell quickly into decay and silted up leaving only shallow depressions to mark its passage. The present harbour dates from the beginning of the seventeenth century when it was decided to abandon the weir entrance site altogether in favour of deeper water and so the new harbour was constructed at a point where the beach shelved more steeply and the tides did not recede as far. In the 1960s I undertook a survey and several excavations to establish where the old foreshore was and where the pre-promenade shingle ridges lay. The original weir harbour opened into two main basins, one at the bottom of the Avenue on the site of Jubilee Gardens and the other where Quay Street is presently at its widest and where the secondary harbour complex was sited.

The word haven, locally associated with a weir harbour, remained in use to describe the area between the two basins and where there was a landing beach. This location was protected by a stone groyne and here it was that timber and stone cargoes were run in on the beach which practice continued until the 1860s. The haven beach was an important site and its name was preserved for us in the Beachhaven Hotel which was built close by. Access straight onto the beach from Ridler's Yard was left open and remained so until the present sea wall was built. In this sheltered corner many vessels spent their last days.

At Porlock Weir it was the Worthy Water that scoured out a sheltered bed within the shingle ridge. Plunging swiftly to meet the coast almost at right angles the stream swung to the east for some distance before finding its way through an easier passage near the present dock gates. Captain William Row's chart of Porlock Bay from early in the eighteenth century clearly shows the Worthy Water charging the *Bason or Wett Dock* before issuing through the dock gates. There has been some conjecture as to whether the large pond immediately behind the chesil bank below the village of Porlock was the remains of Porlock's harbour. On early maps this pond is fed by Porlock Ford Water, West Porlock Water and Porlock Town Brook. This is very similar to the situation at Slapton Ley in South Devon where a body of fresh water is held behind a prominent shingle ridge. At Porlock there are remains of a man-made exit through the shingle but no clear evidence that this was made to support the entry of vessels other than very small boats at high tide. Like Slapton and Abbotsbury in Dorset there is evidence that this area was preserved as a swannery and fishponds and personally, I don't think that port facilities would have been duplicated so close together.

Lynmouth and Watchet developed differently as their harbours were built into and extended from stream beds that exited straight into the sea. All these harbours were protected from the westerlies but it was to be the north-easterly blows that caused the greatest damage over the centuries.

Always popular, peaceful and untroubled sanctuaries compared with the busier ports of Bridgwater or even Watchet, Porlock Weir and Lynmouth were just large enough to satisfy the limited domestic traffic necessitated by an isolated agricultural region like West Somerset and North Devon. Certainly Minehead and Watchet traded with larger vessels which ventured much further afield than little Porlock Weir and Lynmouth smacks, ketches and fishing craft. Since its discovery by poets and artists in the romantic age the area has attracted attention from several well-known writers and painters. My favourite is Charles Napier Hemy (1841-1917) who was working along this coast from the mid 1880s in a converted fishing boat. He painted a splendid picture in oils of Porlock Weir entitled 'The Setting Forth' and depicting a little square-sterned smack leaving the harbour with Hurlestone Point in the background.

From Watchet came Captain Thomas Chidgey (1855-1926) who painted hundreds of fine vessel portraits (see below) and dozens of studies of Watchet harbour. Later, Munnings and Carruthers Gould left an exciting and vivid record of their close involvement with the local coastal landscape. From the mid-nineteenth century however paintings were supplemented by the advent of photography and a new means of historical verification was born.

Looking at old pictures, water-colours as well as oils, that depict these little ports I have often been impressed and saddened by the accuracy on the one hand and the artists' licence on the other. An artist like Charles Napier Hemy knew his vessels well and small individual differences in rig are meticulously represented. There is little doubt that the vessel leaving Porlock Weir in the painting mentioned above is John Lewis's smack *Dolphin*. The artist was equally meticulous in the background to his fishing and shipping scenes so that although 'The Setting Forth' does not give any details of the port where it was painted it is possible to identify its whereabouts by the familiar outline of Hurlestone Point in the distance. However, a number of artists, perhaps more interested in composition, were inclined to alter significant features on their canvasses thus negating any value in considering the work as historical evidence. Such paintings, even naive ones, have significance and often yield interesting contemporary details but very great care has to be exercised if the painting is to be accepted as a document purporting to give accurate historical information. Because a feature is on a painting and that painting is old does not mean to say that it was there at all. This is where the photograph comes into its own.

The photograph is a slice of frozen time. Sometimes it is possible accurately to pinpoint the exact month a building was destroyed or a crane arrived on the quayside simply because the photographer pencilled a date on the back of the print. Ideally it would be wonderful if a range of photographers spent years recording everything that moved and a lot of things that didn't from the advent of the art until the present day and then catalogued them all away with dates and information. This ideal world does not exist but there are thousands of photographs of Porlock Weir, Minehead and Watchet, hundreds of which can be dated to within a decade and presenting unique and valuable data.

I started collecting old pictures and photographs of this region about 1950. At first it was a wide, general collection including moorland, village and farm but as time passed I found that my love of things nautical dictated a focus on the ports of the area and soon I found myself confining my interest to collecting material that related to the Exmoor ports. Luckily in the fifties there was the opportunity to talk to many of the characters that were born in the little coastal townships and villages of the region in the last decades of the nineteenth century and worked out of these ports in fishing boats and sailing craft. I was fortunate to have been able to take photographs that I had unearthed to them to find out the names of vessels and people that appeared in them. Often I was able to hear at first hand stories and anecdotes that had their origins in the daily drama of these tiny commercial outlets. Soon I had a good nucleus of material that spanned the years 1860-1960 and was able to take this along to groups and individuals for them to verify or reject the growing bank of data that had accumulated with each picture. Some of these expeditions were nothing short of exhilarating. On one occasion I was kept up half the night listening to a Watchet schooner skipper telling of a classic race in half a gale between his two-masted tops'l schooner and a newish steamer from Bristol. On another occasion when visiting Bernard Perkins, landlord of The Ship Inn at Porlock Weir

in those days, he pulled out a wonderful old family photograph album that showed Clifford Perkins' work as a youthful photographer in 1906. Clifford's work around the Weir was remarkable because he was interested in making a record of the cottages, vessels and characters of his day.

Family photographs from the Victorian and Edwardian eras often give us more information than the photographer was aware of. I have pictures that show vessels and crews that were lost very shortly afterwards and these pictures become valuable as a last record. For example, the French schooner *La Mouette* ran aground on Small Beach to the east of Hurlstone Point on 12 February 1913 and was photographed half a dozen times by local photographers and naughty boys who had crept on board to see what they could steal. I have several of these in my collection and they show the progressive destruction of this fine craft as she failed to get off and eventually was broken up. Certainly this is the last record of this graceful vessel. Interestingly a picture taken in 1933 of the dock at Porlock Weir by a Great Western Railway photographer shows the water tank of *La Mouette* rusting away on the shingle where it continued to lie for another two decades.

For me, the photograph became a window into the past through which I could glimpse something of what it was like to be a part of Victorian or Edwardian Exmoor. I spent hours with a magnifying glass going over each inch of a photograph looking for clues that would establish further authentic detail. Sometimes I would blow the photograph up as much as I could until I felt I could almost walk into it. Other times, by enlarging, reducing, cutting, pasting and copying it was possible to recreate hundreds of metres of street or dock from a particular viewpoint at a specific time. This book is as much about the use and value of the photograph as historical source material as it is a selection of some of the interesting pictures from my collection on the coast.

Predominantly the material that awaits discovery by collectors was produced by commercial photographers, particularly small local firms and by interested private individuals who might have been enthusiastic about ornithology, arborology or geology. I shall say little of the large national firms of commercial photographers whose collections are, in general, fairly well known. The Frith collection, for example, has stimulated several recent books and thematic essays. The problem here is either that of the availability of less commercially attractive material or if the whole collection has passed into private hands, sections of it may be out of the public domain altogether. Sometimes after the removal of thematic material and the subsequent publication of a book the remainder of a prominent national collection may be auctioned off and other photographic essays are published. After several years of this it becomes very difficult to find out just who owns the material concerned with the smaller fishing ports for example.

The problem of discovery and of ensuring the survival of commercially made photographs of use to local collectors and historians arises in an acute form with the small local firms who existed in considerable numbers before the First World War but who, in many cases, went out of business after some decades or were taken over by larger firms. Collectors interested in finding photographs produced by these small firms would be well advised to approach the extant local photographers to see what collections they might have acquired. I have discovered that some current businesses still hold important material from the earliest days of photography either through direct descent or through the present firm holding the negatives of defunct enterprises. Next the study of local business and trade directories, old advertisements and newspapers for earlier times may give leads to firms which are no longer in business but whose material may be in the possession of other firms or surviving members of the families concerned. Some urgency exists in this matter since, as with other kinds of small business records, irreplaceable materials are constantly being lost or hidden from view. One such example concerns the photographic collection of Clement E. Kille of Minehead. Clement had his studio at the top of his premises in Friday Street and he housed his resulting hoard of several thousand boxed and numbered negatives, mostly in quarter-plate size, in a little windowless box room behind the studio. The earliest photographs dated from 1912 and his most prolific period came in the inter-war years when he became well-known for his excellent sepia studies of the region which he sold in the shop below. The subject matter was wide but confined geographically to West Somerset. There were several boxes relating to shipping and the local ports and some delightful shots of Porlock Weir and Minehead in the 1930s. After Mr Kille's death the shop changed hands twice but remained a commercial photographers the most recent of whom specialised in portraiture and only kept a limited number of topographical postcards for the tourist trade. When again the shop changed hands the business of photography was wound up for ever and the collection of plates, along with all the ancient impedimenta and accumulated equipment of the last fifty years, was disposed of at the tip beyond the gas works at Minehead. Being well packaged there is just the chance that some of these plates remain intact several feet under the present turf. Before its unhappy end early in the sixties I became familiar with the extent of this collection and was allowed to rummage to my heart's content within this local archive taking selections downstairs for the current owner to make copies for me. I was not prepared however for the vandalism which then took place and I confess to being a criminal for as the whole lot was being transported to the rubbish heap I climbed on to the lorry and managed to save one or two boxes before being told to get off and mind my own business. Incidentally, this was not the first time that I have managed to rescue material from the same tip. Clement's work was artistic and many of his studies taking advantage of low evening light or the sharp contrast of light and shade remain in local houses. He was particularly fond of vessels and could be found standing up to his ankles in the harbour mud waiting to catch the light from behind the hull of the *Orestes* as the tide receded in Minehead harbour. It is extremely sad that this man's legacy was destroyed as it was and only a few negatives remain.

Then there are the collections in private hands, in family albums and boxes. These are often of great interest although their quality can be highly variable. Local enquiry by personal contact with old established families, particularly those with local maritime connections, is of great value and it was here that I was to discover some of my richest material. Next, the insertion of advertisements in local newspapers or by a notice in the local library can yield dividends. Experience indicates that it is generally helpful if the collector makes clear the reasons for his or her enquiries and that he wishes only to copy rather then to secure possession of the photograph. The owner will need to be satisfied that due acknowledgement will be made should the photograph appear in any paper or article.

Cost obviously has a bearing on searches for material. The searcher may wish simply to build up a private collection for his or her own use with the idea of the eventual deposit in a public archive or library and be willing and able to meet the cost involved. Should the collector be interested in sharing the findings with the general pubic through the medium of a national or local publication the costs of research may be recovered through the publishers. Should, as can happen with important finds, the expense of acquisition proves exorbitant, then the best line for the researcher is to bring the finds to the attention of local or national libraries, research bodies, universities, colleges or even schools. I found that the University of Exeter was not only interested in some of my findings but published them in a booklet, *Exeter University Papers in Economic History,* 1972.

Collecting the photographs of course is not enough in itself. Enquirers should do their best to date the photographs and to collect as much useful contemporary data about the subject of the picture as possible. Here, personal enquiry, particularly of the older inhabitants, examination of the local newspaper archives, local council records, local publications, guide books, maps and photographs that are of known date and subject, are all ways of helping in the overall identification and confirmation of the material in question. This can be very exciting detective work and where I have had the greatest pleasure.

Certainly you will need to satisfy the basic following questions. Where was the picture taken? Is it clearly a picture of Porlock Weir, for example, even if it is taken from an obscure angle or shows a building that you may not be familiar with? Once I found a picture of some harbour buildings, long pulled down, wrongly titled by the photographer himself who lived in the town. You will need to know your area well and to have walked every footpath and alleyway so that these obscure angles do not fool you despite the growth of trees in the last fifty years or so or the complete destruction of once prominent walls, sheds and cottages that may have been removed in order to widen the road for modern traffic. Where did this photograph come from? What was the size and type of the original? You may not think this very important but if it is a full plate copy then this is most likely to be of commercial origin and there could well be more taken from close by at the same time. Some firms specialised in producing packs of half a dozen flimsy sepia pictures of a harbour or seaside and the finding of one can point to the existence of others. If it was originally a commercial product what is the reference number? Again if the firm's archives are still in existence the number below and above could be interesting to you and you might be able to find it. Who took the picture and what was the name of the firm at the time? What is known of the photographer? What are his dates? What was the reason for taking the picture? Sometimes there was a very good reason for taking a particular picture on a particular day that is not so apparent today and sometimes a picture is taken on the spur of the moment to capture a vivid scene taking place before the photographer's very eyes. This happened on the occasion when a stag was driven out to sea at Porlock Weir and I have a graphic record of the dead stag on the shingle surrounded by onlookers. One photograph I have been searching for over forty years is a vital one for the port of Minehead. I know that several pictures were taken on the occasion of the launch of the Minehead tops'l schooner *Perriton* from the beach at the bottom of Blenheim Road in 1881. There is a well-written account of this in the *West Somerset Free Press* and several eye-witness accounts but no-one has ever come up with an extant copy of any of the photographs taken on that day. That is unless you know differently! Finally the most important of all is the date of the photograph as this can allow the researcher to make definitive statements about historical events.

It is always exciting to link documents and papers from a particular date to a photograph of the same time. Sometimes it is only when the added evidence from a dated negative is brought into the debate that the often much-embroidered truth can be established. Verbal tradition can often distort and usually does when the reputation of a region is at stake. A case in question is the famous memorial nameboard of vessels and masters belonging to the port of Watchet which is to be found in the Watchet Council Chambers. Compiled from memory it gives the names and vastly increased tonnages of Watchet's fleet in the last century thus considerably enlarging the port's importance as a harbour for large sea-going sailing vessels. Only when the actual harbour papers, receipts and dues are consulted for key years and compared with photographs of the named vessels can an accurate picture be shown of each vessel's tonnage, type and rig. It is no less interesting to note that most of Watchet's sailing ships were modest ones engaged mainly in the coastal trade. I have photographs of most of them and documents relating to their size, tonnage and history. It transpires that the famous board quoted in many publications is in error.

Another local story concerns the last vessel to be built at Porlock Weir. On more than one occasion I have heard that this was a large vessel constructed on the shingle bank adjacent to the dock. Luckily there was a photograph of this event and I was able to take it to folk who were present at the launch so that the people in the picture could be identified. She was a fishing boat built and launched inside the dock by the Pollard brothers for Captain Smith of Minehead. The squire himself was present as were several local characters. She was christened *Rosa* and proved to be a good sea boat.

Where the Exmoor ports are concerned, during the period of the late nineteenth and early twentieth centuries, three photographers stand out as having, through their work, provided us with valuable source material although I shall specifically mention others. They are:

James Date, Photographer, Watchet 1807-1895

Herbert Hole, Photographer, Watchet and Williton 1836-1900

Clifford Perkins, Student, Porlock Weir 1894-1910.

Date established himself as a commercial photographer and was active in the region from 1860 until 1885. Hole, the first of three generations of photographers to work in West Somerset, was active from 1865 until his death whilst Perkins, as an amateur, was only active for two years following 1906.

As far as can be established, Porlock Weir and Minehead were visited only once by Date about 1874/5 in his workaday capacity of photographer. He took several pictures which were mounted in an album and kept as a record. This book still exists although I have not seen it for some while now and it has probably changed hands. Occasionally some of Date's plate glass negatives turn up and I once had the pleasure of owning six of them. They bear scrutiny and will stand almost endless enlarging, a tribute to Victorian lens manufacturers and the workmanship involved in making large full plate tripod cameras. These early cameras used in the sixties and seventies had an amazing depth of field and although the figures had to stand very still the landscape came off very well indeed.

Hole travelled the coast several times, the last time in 1898 when he took several excellent pictures with his half plate camera intending them for sale as postcards. He laid down an amazing collection of pictures which was added to by his son and his grandson in turn. This archive was made available to enthusiasts who called at Mr Herbert H. Hole's studio and shop in Long Street, Williton and I have spent many happy hours searching for all the shipping negatives he had stored in cardboard boxes on the shelves in the little room behind the shop. In the late fifties Michael Bouquet used some of these photographs in his book *No Gallant Ship* published by Hollis and Carter in 1959. He also used others in his *Westcountry Sail* published by David and Charles in 1971. Luckily this archive of valuable negatives did not go to the tip when Mr Hole wound up the business but was sold to Michael Bouquet whose family I believe still have it.

Without a doubt, the best photographs of Porlock Weir were taken by Clifford Perkins, then twelve years old, who took to photography as a hobby in the summer of 1906. Clifford's brother Bernard inherited the album that was prepared for the interest of the guests who stayed at the Ship Inn, of which their father was licensee, during the seasons of 1906 and 1907. Clifford also prepared wall charts of photographs of various sizes and went to the trouble of featuring not only the cottages, streets and vessels of the little port but also the interesting characters that lived there in those years. In the early summer of 1907 he was particularly thrilled to meet a photographer of Friths, commercial photographers, who was in the region updating this large firm's portfolio of postcards for sale to the summer visitors. Clifford enthusiastically worked alongside this man and the result was that he featured in one of Frith's best-selling postcards of the dock gates. This gentleman did much to encourage Clifford and told him that upon agreeing a particular view he could take the photograph for the firm and so it was that Clifford could proudly point to one of Frith's popular postcard series and say, 'I took that one' Unfortunately Clifford died of rheumatic fever at Taunton school in 1910 at the of sixteen and the village was the poorer for a talented lad who left behind him a valued and unique record of Porlock Weir in Edwardian times. Clifford's brother Bernard went on to become landlord of the Ship Inn himself and was a passionate lover of local coastal sail. Before the days when it would be foolhardy to exhibit original oil paintings on the wall of a public house, Bernard hung his superb collection of paintings by Captain Thomas Chidgey of Watchet and Carruthers Gould of Porlock on the walls of the public bar. Bernard loved to talk of the days when he and his brother and sister used to play among the host of rotting hulks that lay within the dock in those days. That he allowed me to root among his private family papers and photographs was an indication of his friendly genial spirit and generosity.

Through the medium of the work of these and other photographers like Alfred Vowles and Clement Kille and the supplementary and explanatory information that can be gained from personal enquiry and other sources it is possible to obtain more than a glimpse of the character and development of these ports in late Victorian and Edwardian times. It becomes clear that they were the scene of many activities relating to shipping and fishing whilst a tourist business can be observed to gain momentum as the years pass.

What follows is a small selection of photographs taken of these havens at different times during this period and some of the stories and anecdotes that were passed to me over forty years ago. Those characters whose great grandparents were smugglers and who were able to tell me some of the adventures they had evading the local Customs officers made me promise that I would never tell during their lifetimes because they still feared that there might be some repercussions for past crimes. I'm still keeping quiet about some of the stories.

An excellent guide to who was living where and following what occupation, is to be found in directories like the one below. *Pigot's* of 1830 tells us, for instance, that the Anchor at Porlock Weir was managed by John Peelsford at that time and that the landlord of the Ship Inn was Hugh Poole confirming that both inns were open for business in 1830, not that this is any surprise for both buildings have parts that are extremely old. Directories are also useful for establishing which family names and occupations extend back to the time of the directory. Although *Pigot's Directory* for 1830 is from before the

advent of commercial photography, it is nevertheless a useful tool to have at hand as it sketches a picture of the locality and an understanding of the immediate background to the commercial interests in the region at that time.

A glimpse at the RAF oblique shot of Porlock Weir in its entirety shows the extent of the original enclosed area. The old stream bed is evident as is the original exit point. Aerial shots like this one taken in 1947 often yield valuable information and can support photography on the ground.

PORLOCK WEIR

PORLOCK WEIR

fig. 1

1. The approach to the village

This photograph was taken by Clifford Perkins in 1908. It is a posed shot where the instructions given went something like this, 'I want you both to be looking at the dog while I get the village into the background.' His brother Bernard is sitting on the railings that mounted the new sea wall and the dog has turned to look at the photographer. The picture is interesting because it shows the newly established approach road to the Weir which was made up in 1894. Previous to this it was only a muddy track across the top of the shingle ridge which was often washed away by high spring tides. The picture shows four of the strong timber groynes which were erected thirty years earlier in an attempt to prevent longshore drift dragging pebbles into the mouth of the little dock. In the extreme right of the picture can be seen the continuation of this shingle bank which sweeps on to the westward to culminate in Gore Point. Porlock Weir lies at the extreme westerly point of the sweep of Porlock Bay which is bounded by a chesil beach very similar in construction to the one in Dorset. Very occasionally this is breached by floods or heavy storms and the area lying immediately behind it is flooded. Directly behind Bernard Perkins is the depression called Oyster Perch, in those days a permanent pond where in the time when the Weir supported a small oyster dredging fleet, the oysters were kept before their sale at the local fish market which was situated on the site of the present car park. The house on the left of the picture is still called Oyster Perch built as it was opposite this pond.

2. The Pollard brothers' houses on the beach road

The sea front road was only built and surfaced and a sea wall built in 1894 before which date it was little more than a rough track along the top of the shingle ridge protected from the sea by a strong wooden barrier which kept the shingle in place. The old road to the Weir, established for a thousand years, ran along the boundary of the wood on higher ground and is bordered by a famous row of fifteenth and sixteenth century cottages and smallholdings. This shingle ridge path is found on several old maps and plans of the area but it never achieved any significance until the last decade of the nineteenth century when it became the wider and more easily negotiated route into the village. Once the beach road became a viable propo-

fig. 2

sition and plans were afoot to build a sea wall in stone to replace the timber structure, Noah and William Pollard put a major part of their capital from vessel sales and work into a pair of stone-built semi-detached houses right opposite the perch or pond where they used to store dredged oysters before sale. Called 'Oyster Perch' and 'Mizpah' they remain today much as built. Both Noah and William were warned that they were building in a dangerous place and ought to consider building them on higher ground. They knew however, that severe flooding only occurred roughly once every hundred years and gambled that the new wall, when built, would protect their assets. They were right and when the next hurricane force gale hit the village it was 1910 and the sea wall did indeed prevent the houses from damage although their garden walls fronting the road were totally demolished.

fig. 3

3. The great gale of 1910

There were several photographs taken in the village illustrating the damage done by this gale which was without doubt the worst this century and responsible for more harm than the 1990 gale. It washed walls out, damaged cottages, smashed doors and windows and even flooded the bedrooms of the houses in the extreme right of this picture. Without a sea wall the shingle bank would certainly have been breached and the roadway washed away. Dennis Corner in his fascinating book *Porlock in Those Days* tells some of the stories about the cottagers who were almost washed out of their homes. Noah Pollard was always proud of the fact that his flag pole survived

and put it down to the fact that it was a vessel's topmast, well used to a stiff blow. His brother put it down to the fact that when it was put up three quarters of it was underground. This picture, which is probably by Alfred Vowles, shows all that is left of a wall adjacent to the Pollards' houses.

4. A Trading smack awaiting entry to the dock

Although there is a lack of contemporary detail in this picture the condition of the timber shoring to the shingle bank in the centre of the picture points to it being some time in the 1880s and possibly 1885. The name of the vessel is not visible but she

fig. 4

fig. 5

is a little square-sterned trading smack and answers very closely to a description of Captain John Lewis's smack *Dolphin* which he used in his coal business from the dock. *Dolphin* made regular trips across the channel to Welsh ports for coal and culm. Four of the oyster fishing vessels can be seen tied up beneath Turkey Cottages. Navigators will be interested to note the channel marker on the extreme right of the picture. The source of this picture is Bernard Perkins again and Bernard did not know who took it although he thought it might have been an early commercial picture. He could be right and it may well be an early Frith print as it is certainly an artistic interpretation of the port and the photographer had obviously waited for a dramatic high tide.

5. The Anchor Hotel from the harbour wall

This viewpoint was also popular with commercial photographers and this is a prime example of a posed photograph by a professional. The original [58367] could well be a Frith but it could equally be another of the larger national firms photographing around the coast. The historian's eye is at first directed to the buildings and vessels but the characters are all well known villagers. From left to right we have Tom Pugsley, a local fisherman and boat owner, Noah Pollard, fisherman and boat-builder and Captain Tom Perkins, sailing ship master and part owner of several local vessels. The little lad sitting up so smartly for the photographer has not been identified but as this photograph is likely to be from 1907 or 1908 there may be

someone alive today who can recognise him. Among the vessels is *The Laureate*, the last of the oyster dredgers and a vessel we shall meet again as this story unfolds. Other vessels include *The Nancy Lee, The Dove,* and *The Mayflower.* A prominent building in the centre right of the photograph half clad with ivy was built as a warehouse and store. Today it is a shop and a dwelling but when I was a young man a coastguard had his office on the ground floor and parts of the building were still in use as a store. Living on the ground floor was a friendly local character called Sid Stenner whose claim to fame was that he served on board *HMS Montagu* when she went aground on the Great Shutter Rock, Lundy Island in 1906. He was much in demand as the maker of intricate bell ropes and was the subject of much local teasing over the *Montagu* incident. Locals even went so far as to fabricate an official looking certificate attributing the blame for the wreck to him! The photograph was taken from halfway along the stone quay or harbour which was built with its back into the shingle bank in an attempt to provide shelter for vessels before they entered the dock. This mediaeval cob harbour is very similar to the original parts of those at Minehead and Watchet although this one probably predates that at Minehead as there are records of its repair in the fifteenth century. It was also built to protect the entry to the dock before the dock gates were erected. The entrance to the dock itself was likely to have been established in stone and mortar at an earlier date and the stream, when it flowed out from this entrance, would have been the main method of keeping the channel clear.

fig. 6

6. The Anchor Hotel

As far back as written records go there were two inns at Porlock Weir, the Anchor and the Ship and both can be seen in this photograph, although the Ship is tucked away behind the white cob cottage on the left. The Anchor started life as a two-storey cob building with a thatched roof which today is seen in the centre section of the hotel. The next development was the twin-gabled extension with double bays on the right which served the premises well in the years when the tourist trade was establishing itself.

7. The Anchor Hotel circa 1920

This shot shows the Anchor Hotel following the addition of a second double-gabled extension to the east which was erected in 1902 replacing the thatched building. The date can still be made out on the original cast iron guttering under the valley between the two gables. You will notice that the thatch of the original building has been replaced with tiles but the old chimney stack remains. The pattern of the eastern wing broadly follows the first extension, although the window shapes, following contemporary architectural trends, are now horizontal rather than vertical. Notice the row of houses in the

fig. 7

top right of the picture, which appeared in the second decade of the twentieth century.

8. The foreshore to the east of the dock gates

This photograph, taken about 1908, shows the secondary development to the premises now known as the Cottage Hotel. This house was the fourth in the village to sport a flagstaff, the others being at Oyster Perch, the Ship Inn and the Anchor. High in the centre of the picture can be seen the cot-

fig. 8

tages that line the old road into the village which descends by the side of the Cottage Hotel. This picture also shows the rear of the cottages that were built on the shingle ridge itself, although I suspect that bedrock is not far below. Legend has it that the row extended further to the west, covering the ground which was once a fish market and is presently a car park. These houses, of similar cob construction to the ones that still exist in the rows known as Gibraltar and Turkey were thought to have been destroyed in a titanic gale early in the seventeenth century. When one examines these cottages, they are found to be very similar to the ones in Quay Street, Minehead or close to the harbour at Watchet and they represent the earliest surviving artisan dwellings inhabited mainly by the fishing and trading community. The foundations and much of the walls were constructed from beach stones with the upper stories often built from cob which was a mixture of mud, dung, animal hair, straw and lime, and when dried out took on the consistancy of brick and has lasted for centuries. Usually limewashed annually and thatched repeatedly, they were extremely durable, warm and watertight. It is highly likely that these limewashed thatched cottages were originally put up in the fourteenth century, replacing earlier timber and thatch buildings.

9. Vessels awaiting entry to the dock

This photograph of Porlock Weir by Clifford Perkins represents the little port at the zenith of the Edwardian era, a useful local outlet for domestic industry and an infant resort growing in popularity. The smack *M & E* and a large ketch await entry to the dock. The *M & E* has just dropped an anchor over the stern to secure her from swinging across the entry. You can see the splash. The *M & E* was a regular trader to Porlock Weir mainly in the cross-channel trade with coal. There are three pleasure boats lying in the approach, Tom Pugsley's *Jessamine, The Nancy Lee*, and the *EJT*. Standing on the side of the dock entry is a crowd of sightseers. They will have a little while to

fig. 9

fig. 10

wait as there is not yet enough water to take the vessels in. This was a hot day in the summer of 1906 and the angle of the sun and the ladies' parasols tell us that it is the afternoon.

10. The dock gates

These are the old dock gates which were replaced in 1913 when the timber had become rotten. The gates were hand-operated by chain winding gear. There was also an outlet under the harbour wall visible beneath the cottages to the right of the picture. These dock gates were as vulnerable as any lock gates and were constantly in need of repair. They were repaired and rebuilt in 1878 but needed extensive work in 1913 when the dock was cleared of wrecks and the entrance dredged out and widened.

This photograph shows the oyster fishing vessel *Laureate* at close quarters. She is seen here lying in the dock approach. *Laureate* was the last remaining oyster boat of quite a large fleet. She was to be refitted early in 1914 in an attempt to relocate and dredge the local beds which had been abandoned some twenty years earlier. At one time there were extensive beds off Porlock Weir and the resulting harvest found its way as far afield as the London market. Following the arrival of the railway at Minehead in 1874 a fast rail link meant that Porlock oysters could be on the dinner table the same day that they were caught.

Although paper records of the oyster fishing fleet are rare to non-existent, some photographs show these craft and the way that they were rigged. The names are from verbal tradition and are therefore unreliable yet probably contain most of the prominent boats. They are *Lively, Albion, Carmella, Trial, Tanner's Dog, Oceana, Robin Hood, Charlotte, Blessing, Towser, Teazer* and the *Undaunted*. Some of these were smack-rigged with a running bow-sprit and a single pole mainmast like the *Laureate*. Others carried a pole mizzen to carry a steadying sail over the stern. This latter was raked aft. They were fine sea boats, deep hulled with a pronounced sheer. They were decked-in for'ard as far as the first thwart, carried two further thwarts midships with ample stern seating for comfortable sailing. Most had a narrow square stern. Although the Ministry was interested in reviving the Porlock oyster fishing industry and subsidised the refitting of the *Laureate* the scheme failed and it was surmised that the original beds had been washed out by successive winter storms and the accompanying heavy ground swells. *Laureate* however remained at the Weir although she was eventually laid up in the dock and abandoned after she had become too expensive to repair. The other vessel is the *Nancy Lee*, a gaff-rigged cutter yacht with running bow-sprit and dipping topmast. She was used mainly for pleasure and taking out the visitors who came to stay at The Ship Inn and The Anchor Hotel. The boy in the pulling boat may be Clifford Perkins. He is holding an oar in the position for sculling which was the traditional way of moving boats around the harbour. This photograph dates from the summer of 1907 when Clifford was taking photographs himself for display in the inn.

11. Opening the sluice gates

Always spectacular was the opening of the paddles in the base of the lock gates thus ejecting the contents of the dock

fig. 11

with all the force of the weight of water behind the gates. This was done periodically to keep the main channel as clear as possible. The problem was however that the channel made a dog-leg before emerging into the sea and whereas this sluicing cleared the area immediately beyond the dock gates most of the material so cleared came to rest fifty yards or so down the entry to the dock. Sometimes this accumulated shingle needed clearing in order to accommodate the vessels engaged in the coastal trade. If one looks closely at the centre of the picture one can see two men raising the paddles by means of a mechanical windlass.

12. The sloop Elizabeth Anne

This vessel was owned by Mr Clarke of Lynch who had a considerable business dealing with limestone, coal and culm and timber. He was the owner of several vessels and as Porlock Weir was his nearest port they were usually to be found there. The *Elizabeth Anne* was a big strong square-sterned vessel whose boom was as long as the smaller vessel secured alongside her. These large craft were the final word in the development of the single-masted cargo carrier and it was not long before they were superseded by the versatile ketch. Some of these larger smacks carried huge areas of sail and were extremely powerful vessels. Many were tiller-steered and could prove difficult to handle with small crews which is why so many of them were converted to ketches by the addition of a mizzen-mast when an average crew of two or three men and a boy could cope adequately. The practice of off-loading cargo by hand over the

fig. 12

side can be seen here as a cargo of Welsh limestone lies ready to be collected by cart and hauled to the limekiln behind the dock. Burning lime for the acid moorland soils was considered the best way of balancing the soils of the region and the practice extended until the production of more modern bagged fertilisers and additives which could be transported by rail and motor lorry.

13. The smack M & E preparing to enter the dock

This is another fascinating photograph taken by Clifford Perkins in the summer of 1906. It shows the work-a-day element of the little port as a vessel prepares to enter the dock. There are hobblers in attendance and they can be seen assisting at the stern of the vessel. One of the hobblers has gone aboard and will, presumably, offer advice on the actual entry. You may think that with the dock entrance only a few hundred yards from deep water the skipper of an incoming vessel might tackle the exercise himself but with shingle that could shift on almost any tide it would be imprudent to ignore local assistance. Furthermore as the hobblers were also local fishermen and stevedores it would be counter-productive to attempt to do without them. The office of hobbler was jealously guarded in all the little West Somerset ports and in Minehead and Watchet as well as Porlock Weir the ancient right of assisting vessels in and out of harbour brought an income and carried status.

fig. 13

The *M & E* was a small traditionally built Welsh sloop and is seen here rigged as built with a running bow-sprit, gaff mainsail and topmast. At a time when many smacks and ketches were fitting auxiliary engines and losing their topmasts, the *M & E* continued under sail alone. She was owned and skippered by Walter Webber of Minehead who ran her with the help of his brother Jesse. Many was the adventure experienced by this stalwart little craft as it pursued its weekly task of fetching coal from the South Wales coalfields, mainly from the Eley River for Minehead and Porlock Weir. In size she was typical of generations of sloop-rigged craft working in the Channel. Vessels like this were responsible for carrying all commercial cargoes and every domestic appliance from limestone to pianos and were expected to land everything safely where required.

fig. 14

Sometimes these vessels had to nose their way up small creeks or land their cargoes on steeply shelving shingle beaches with little shelter. The picture shows the vessel preparing to stow her recently lowered fores'l under which she has just moved up the channel. She is deeply laden and needs the high water. The gates of the dock are open to receive her. Some years ago a fine replica was built of the *M & E* by an enthusiast. Whilst this craft is still afloat the original *M & E* lies as a wreck below Haverfordwest.

14. The M & E *discharging cargo*

This photograph shows the *M & E* inside the dock, secured alongside the little coal wharf. Her cargo is being unloaded with the help of a whip rigged to a jury gaff on the main mast. The vessel's gaff and boom are rigged outboard by the use of a ladder in order to clear space above the open hatch which can be seen in the centre of the picture. Working on board are Noah Pollard in the stern sheets, Jesse Webber at the winch and Walter Webber helping to off-load. Also on board, would be helpers below bagging up coal by hand – a most unpleasant task.

fig. 15

This is one of Clifford Perkins' pictures and, unlike those taken for commercial purposes, shows village characters at work and records the visit of regular traders like the *M & E*. Pictures of the working day are rare as few working men liked to be caught dirty and sweaty and preferred to pose after they had spruced themselves up. There are several shots of unwilling sea-farers who have covered their faces with their hands or held a cap in the way of the camera lens.

fig. 16

15. The wreck of the M & E

This picture of the *M & E* was taken in the mid-sixties in a little creek below Haverfordwest. The tidelines on her starboard side show that at high water much of her was submerged. There is probably very little of her left now!

16. The Ship Inn

The Ship Inn is a wonderful old building. Bernard Perkins was landlord before taking the Rest and Be Thankful at Wheddon Cross. After he retired to Carhampton he was kind enough to allow me access to his family papers and photographs and to an enormous fund of stories about the Weir which both he and his father had collected since the turn of the century.

The Ship was always very much the village pub and not involved to the same extent with visitors as the Anchor, which boasted the name of hotel. The Ship was popular with visitors, but it also seemed to attract the sailors, the fishermen, the longshoremen, the farmers and the locals.

In the fifties you could pile into the bar at the Ship and enjoy a rich West Country atmosphere orchestrated by Bernard and many of the locals. The walls were covered with vessel portraits and photos of ships and the occasional oil painting left by Carruthers Gould. The pictures were local, the ale was local and the company was local or sea-faring and the bar at the Ship was an example of what an English pub was all about.

17. The party from Cardiff visits the Ship

A regular annual visit to the Weir during the early 1900s was made by John Davis of Cardiff who, using Captain Wallis's

fig. 17

steam tug, brought a party across to the dock, always lunching at the Ship. This became such a regular occurrence that friendships were formed and reciprocal visits made to Wales to the homes of party members. As the oldest inhabitant Jan Pollard was always an honoured guest and can be seen here sporting his white whiskers next to Captain Wallis in the centre of the picture. John Davis stands on the other side of the captain whilst the landlord, Mr Perkins, can be seen with his daughter on the extreme left. This photograph was probably taken shortly before the First World War put an end to the trips.

fig. 18

18. The death of a stag is recorded

Captain Tom Perkins, widely known as an able coastal skipper and master of the ketch *Nautilus*, poses here by the corpse of a deer that he has just landed after collecting it at sea into which it had been hunted earlier in the day. This photograph is probably about 1905/6, although hunt records and local reports in the newspaper would pinpoint it more accurately. There have been several instances of deer preferring to enter the sea rather than face the hounds although this is probably the earliest photograph of such an event.

19. Beelzebub Terrace (Lane Head Cottages)

This row may have been so named because of the large number of psychic occurrences reported over the centuries: hauntings, sightings of ghosts and stories of inexplicable happenings have long been known in the area.

20. Inside the dock

This is a print from one of James Date's glass negatives which was copied in 1964. Date's photography was of a high standard and much of his work was with a full plate camera resulting in pin-sharp definition. His exposures were long which precluded the shooting of movement but where the view was

fig. 19

static, or could be encouraged to be so, the results were excellent. This photograph is likely to have been taken in the mid 1870s probably 1876 when Date visited other villages and townships in the region and certainly before 1878 because it does not show the little bridge put up in 1878 when repairs were being carried out to the dock gates. A timber cargo can be seen awaiting export and limestone can be seen in the right of the picture which has been off-loaded by a vessel from South Wales. It is another piece of evidence showing the commercial nature of the port. On the left of the picture there is a beached and dismasted fishing boat. She is half-decked and built up to afford protection for the crew who would be using

fig. 20

her in the traditional herring season which was between October and Christmas. Behind the fishing boat is a largish hulk which is probably the *Brunswick* which lay there until the harbour was cleared out at the end of 1912 and 1913.

21. The wreck of the Brunswick

This commercially produced sepia flimsy, taken about 1897, was composed at a point 25 yards to the east of picture number 20 and shows the development of the buildings and dock over twenty years. The hulk of the *Brunswick* is still in the same position though she has lost some planking on her port quarter. The largish fishing vessel has gone and in its place there are two others; the double ender *Jane* and a particularly handsome deep hulled open fishing boat with a square stern. During the last fifteen years of the nineteenth century much of the dock was used as a graveyard for derelict and elderly craft. Many of these were the property of 'Farmer John' Redd who could not resist a bargain and was sold several craft that afterwards proved not as good as he had first thought. Some he was able to sell on if the price was right but others were doomed to lie as a source of firewood and spare parts until the harbour was cleared in 1913. At the turn of the century there were above a dozen such craft slowly mouldering away.

fig. 21

fig. 22

22. The smack Ranger and four other craft in the graveyard

This photograph was taken in 1893 and the vessel in the centre is particularly interesting. It not only helps us to date the photograph but shows us the deck arrangements of a small working smack of the nineteenth century before the advent of steam coasters or even auxiliary engines. This little smack of 24 tons, was built in 1797 and registered at Cowes. She had a varied history in several south coast ports before attracting the attention of 'Farmer John' when in Bridgwater who thought she would be ideal for his coal business. He had her delivered to the Weir but discovered that a lot of her planking needed renewing. He had her surveyed and the cost of repairs almost amounted to the cost of another second-hand vessel so while he made up his mind the *Ranger* was hauled well up the dock alongside the *RJW* which lies slightly ahead of her in the photograph. 'Farmer John' also owned the *Herbert*, the *Sophia* and the *Caerleon*, a hopeless sailer and 'a bit like trying to sail a haystack' as one of her skippers remarked. *Caerleon* was one of the last wrecks to remain and can be seen in many photographs gradually deteriorating in the dock. The *Ranger* however was not doomed and was spotted by Captain Pulsford of Minehead who was well able to do the repairs himself and in 1894 he bought her at a bargain price, patched her, took her to Minehead and successfully put her to work in the coastal trade for the next decade. 'Farmer John' was a

great character. He lived at Broomstreet Farm with his sister Elizabeth and drove every day to Porlock Weir where he had a coal business. He was a chain smoker, smoking a sealed tin of fifty per day and could always be found at midday in the Ship Inn having a drink with his lunch. Once when he had a supposed broken leg, and it was in splints and bandages, he left his office at the Weir for his usual midday tipple minus his crutches and was promptly asked where they were. He turned and ran to his office and came back on his crutches.

'Farmer John' was under contract to the Rural District Council in the early 1920s to maintain the road and keep the level of the hedges down. Folk were amused to see him driving along the road in a two-wheeled butt standing bolt upright, reins in one hand and a sickle in the other, slashing out at the overhead branches. For decades he was known for his warm-hearted hospitality and everyone was welcome. The open-hearth fire never went out; long oak poles were inserted into the fire, the rest of the pole lying across the kitchen floor. 'They'll burn shorter', he used to say. One could almost always find on the kitchen table boiled pork and bacon and, in season, cooked herrings. His sister always provided a good drop of home-brewed ale and there was always cider indoors as well.

In the background of the photograph can be seen the limekilns which 'Farmer John' repaired and rebuilt for another of his interests was providing lime for the acid soils of Exmoor and it was he who built the limekiln on the shingle beach below Broomstreet Farm. He made a roadway down through the dense woods of scrub oak, zig-zagging back and forth to make the slope less difficult for the carts to come up from the beach. To anyone who knows this landscape it was a herculean project. The story goes that only one cargo of stone was landed. It had to be unloaded on the beach which consisted of huge boulders and then dragged by hand to the kiln. After being burnt the lime was to be hauled a thousand feet up the lane to the moor. Locals reckoned that it would take half a day to transport half a ton. Needless to say, this scheme failed – partly perhaps because limeburning was already in decline.

23. Captain Henry Pulsford

Captain Henry (Griff) Pulsford lived in nearby Minehead but was a familiar figure in all the West Country seaport towns and indeed in maritime communities of Ireland and much of Western Europe. He epitomised that breed of coastal sailorman that we shall never see again. Surviving into his nineties he was a model of honesty, dignity and strength and all those who remember him treasure their memories of this man and of the many stories that are told about him. He first went to sea at sixteen in 1851 on a voyage to the Baltic. By the age of twenty-two he was master of a vesssel and by twenty-five owner of a number of craft trading out of Minehead. He died in 1931 a t the age of ninety-six.

He faced ruin many times as vessels he owned were either lost or wrecked. The following is from the *West Somerset Free Press* dated 17 October 1891 and I quote, 'Three craft belonging to Captain Henry Pulsford, the *John and Henry*, the *Looe* and the *Prosperous*, which put out from Minehead harbour encountered the force of a great gale that swept the Channel, and the

Prosperous, under Captain A. Baker, drove ashore near Lydney and was battered so badly as to cause her to fill when she drifted off into deep water and sank. Those on board were saved.' The last one was the little smack *Dart* a vessel that was wrecked at Blue Anchor in 1901 whilst running in with a cargo of coal.

24. The launch of the Rosa

This photograph showing the launch of the last craft to be built at Porlock Weir was found amongst family papers by Bernard Perkins in the 1960s. It shows the Pollard brothers

who built her standing next to the boat, James Pulsford with his hand on his hip, the squire Mr Robert Blathwayt in panama hat and Mr George Blathwayt with pipe, the squire's brother. Captain Smith, for whom the *Rosa* was built, is standing in the boat and was probably launched in it. Mr George Blathwayt is leaning against the bows of the old Watchet lifeboat which, after service, was used as a private yacht. The vessel in the background with the life belt secured in the starboard mizzen rigging is 'Farmer John's' *Caerleon*. Opposite on the jetty is a cargo of timber awaiting export. The Pollard brothers were primarily engaged in herring fishing and boat repairs and the *Rosa* was the last complete boat they built. Several vessels were built at Porlock Weir in the closing years of the nineteenth century as the site afforded a sheltered position for both work and launch. Local timber was available and the expertise at hand. Traditionally trunnels (tree nails) came from the scrub oak growing in nearby Culbone Woods and there was a plentiful supply of elm from the vale of Porlock. The smack *John and William* was built here in 1858 by William Pulsford and was a regular trader from Minehead harbour in the Bristol Channel coasting trade. There were three prominent families engaged in seafaring at the Weir. They were the Pugsleys, the Pollards and the Perkins and they were known as the three Ps. Other families so engaged were the Moggridges, the Wards and the Leys, the Marleys and the Manleys. Their names crop up in official documents like Bills of Sale for vessels and part ownerships where several families held a number of shares in a larger vessel. The Bill of Sale still exists for the tops'l schooner *Florence Muspratt* of Chester when Robert Manley of Porlock Weir acquired shares in the vessel from Captain Robert Marley on 23 March 1893. Later documents witnessed that Robert Manley became sole owner of the *Muspratt* having bought out all the shares over a number of years. Robert Manley was not a seafarer but, like many local traders, had an interest in vessels.

25. Jan Pollard

'Doverhay ducks,
Minehead herrings,
Porlock Weir men'
(a saying of the Weir boatmen)

Born in the second decade of the nineteenth century, Jan Pollard in 1906 was much respected as a grand old sailorman and village character. He was included in several formal photographs taken in 1906 and 1907 by Clifford Perkins who thought, like other villagers, that he deserved the recognition and esteem of his years. Jan was a kindly, gentle, humorous, obliging and earnest man and willingly posed for Clifford when Clifford asked him if he would sit for him as the village's oldest inhabitant. Jan smiles and sits on his favourite stone overlooking the dock entrance where he could watch the fishing boats come and go and the trading vessels enter the dock. He is carrying his favourite stick which can be seen in other photographs of him.

26. Seafarers after the fish market

Posing here are Tom Ward, Jesse Webber of the *M & E* and Jim Pulsford who agreed to be photographed by Clifford Perkins in the summer of 1906. Tom Ward's father and grandfather were involved in 'the trade' which meant that they were engaged in evading the duty on specific items entering the country. Even during the Napoleonic wars when we were supposed to be at war with France, a very lucrative business con-

fig. 25

fig. 26

nection was established with ports all around our coast and hundreds of small coastal craft were engaged in bringing in brandy and other contraband to the most inaccessible and remote parts of the coast. In the centre of the picture is Jesse Webber who, with his brother Walter, owned and sailed the little Welsh trading sloop *M & E*. On the right of the picture is Jim Pulsford, notorious for his humour, sharp wit and practical jokes. He would send folk on spurious errands, give visitors erroneous directions which would have them trespassing or wandering into neighbours' gardens and, on several occasions, received money for jobs he had not done leaving other people to sort out the mess. Nevertheless, he was hugely popular and always ready with a joke.

fig. 27

27. *The wooden bridge across the dock*

In 1878 a temporary wooden structure was erected across the dock while the dock gates were out of commission during a refit. It appeared on maps the following year and it remained for many years until finally collapsing some time in the first decade of the present century. In this photograph which is taken well up the dock we can see several wrecks and this of course is why the upper dock area became known as the graveyard before it was cleared between 1912 and 1913.

28. *The ketch* **Mistletoe**

The *Mistletoe*, Official No. 93983 and of twenty three tons reg., was designed and built by David Banks of Oreston, Plymouth in 1890 for Captain Tom Ley who had her especially strengthened for landing cargoes on small rocky beaches. Tom Ley had come to Porlock Weir from Combe Martin where he had established a reputation as a knowledgable coastal skipper. This photograph was taken about the turn of the century by Herbert Henry Hole for his commercial photographic business and shows the *Mistletoe* in splendid condition. She has left the dock after unloading and is secured in the channel before leaving. The Leys sold her on in the 1920s to Messrs G. Heywood and Sons Ltd of Queen Street, Exeter, who immediately fitted her with a 26 horse power engine and put her to work along the south coast.

fig. 28

fig. 29

29. Two ketches and a smack within the dock

This especially clear and detailed photograph was taken by H. H. Hole in 1898. Limestone has been unloaded outside the dock and bricks and tiles are waiting to be loaded in the foreground. By the turn of the century only the coal, limestone and brick-making enterprises remained. The timber trade was dying while flour-milling, rope-making, ship-building, bark-stripping and the cutting of oak for 'chemical wood' had declined almost to extinction. Porlock Weir and Minehead both exported 'chemical wood' from the extensive local woodlands to South Wales where it was used for the production of methyl alcohol by destructive distillation.

30. The tops'l schooner Florence Muspratt

This beautiful two-masted tops'l schooner of 78 tons was owned in Porlock Weir. She was built at Burton Stather in Lincolnshire in 1869 by John Wray and Sons and was once skippered by the famous Captain John Coppack of Connah's Quay. This vessel came down to Robert Marley in Porlock Weir in the March of 1893 for £500. Mr Harry Manley bought a third share in her for £180 and she traded out of the Bristol Channel to the Irish ports until she was drafted into war work at the outbreak of the First World War. In 1897 a further third share was sold to Mr Harry Manley by Captain Thomas Marley, Robert Marley's son, for £175. Then, on the death of Mr Robert Marley, the final third share in the vessel was made over to Mr Harry Manley for £160 and he became

the sole owner of the *Muspratt* from 18 September 1913. Unfortunately, in 1917 she was blown out of the water by a German submarine a few miles north of St Malo. The mate was killed by shell fire. Captain Jack Redd and the rest of the crew made away in the boat and were picked up the following day. The boy on board was Tom Rawle of Quay Street, Minehead and I am grateful to him for giving me an accurate and detailed account of the sinking.

31. Captain Thomas Chidgey's painting of the Florence Muspratt

The *Florence Muspratt* was always much admired although she spent little time at Porlock Weir being better suited to larger ports. The sailor artist Captain Thomas Chidgey of Watchet painted her several times and this painting, still in the Manley family, is now in Sydney, Australia. Captain Chidgey's paintings of local ships were popular with local vessel owners and his pictures survive in their dozens.

32. The great gale of January 1881

This painting by Captain Tom Chidgey depicts a big schooner caught shortened down in the memorable gale of January 1881. Her tops'l is blown out and she is hard pressed under a reefed jib and shortened mains'l. He painted this within the month as evidenced by the newspaper he used to pack the frame. The frame has since succumbed to woodworm but the

fig. 30

fig. 31

fig. 32

painting survives in splendid condition and has now been acquired by the Watchet Museum

33. The ketch Nautilus

Skippered for much of her life by Captains Robert Marley and Thomas Perkins of Porlock Weir this stout little ketch ran a shopping service for local traders in Porlock and Lynmouth running up to Bristol on a regular basis. When she wasn't shopping she carried coal and limestone like many of her contemporaries. She is seen here beached at Lynmouth.

34. The ketch Three Sisters *at the Weir*

This veteran vessel was built in 1800 at Plymouth as a smack although by the time she came into the ownership of Captain Tom Ley of Porlock Weir she had been converted to a ketch. Her port of registry was Cowes and she was widely known as the *Three Sisters* of Cowes. Her history has been well researched and she was lost off the Longships in 1921. There are many photographs of the *Three Sisters* in the dock and this shot is probably among the last to be taken of her entering and leaving the dock.

35. High tide in the dock 1906

We have Clifford Perkins to thank for this shot which shows James Pollard sculling a boat through the dock entrance. James

fig. 33

fig. 34

fig. 35

ahead of a ketch while a smack is tied up alongside. The barge looks out of place among the more familiar west coast ketches and smacks. It is likely to have come for local tiles which were in demand by specialist builders in London. The *Caerleon* is seen in the right of the picture. The whole picture is ably composed giving the impression of a crowded harbour scene.

36. The dock at Porlock Weir

This is an example of a commercially produced postcard from a firm some distance away from West Somerset. It is possibly by Sweetman and Son of Tonbridge Wells but the original is not to hand. The negative number is 3516 and the photograph

is looking up at Clifford who is standing right on the dock gate. An expert will recognise that James is deliberately posing to allow for the exposure. An east coast sprits'l barge is secured

fig. 36

is entitled *Porlock Docks*, a mistake that a local photographer would not make. By carefully looking at the rest of the picture it seems that it was taken about 1895/6. Although the photographer has chosen a still, bright summer day, the long exposure has picked up movement on the surface of the water to the right of the picture between the piles of limestone.

The vessel on the right of the picture is the ketch *Penguin* of Beaumaris. Sadly the *Penguin* was lost in November 1901. Throughout the era of sail seamanship was of paramount importance and one slip made by a member of the crew could end in disaster, and often did. What happened to the ketch *Susanna* on the morning of 14 December 1906 is a fair illustration of the dangers encountered in the everyday drama of local sail. Under the command of Captain Tom Rawle, she was bound for Porlock Weir with coal out of Lydney. She made the Weir in the late evening. Having missed the tide she brought up in Porlock Bay lying between the Gore and Hurlestone Point in a safe enough anchorage to wait for sufficient water to take her into the dock but a rising wind from the west sou'west brought high seas and the crew became anxious. They waited for as long as they were able until they realised it would be impossible to get in and then decided to run for Minehead harbour. Getting sail on, they came back on the flood and reached the harbour two hours before high water. The *Susanna* secured astern of the ketch *Orestes* which was moored at the post in the centre of the harbour. When the weather deteriorated the crew of the *Orestes* decided to move their vessel into a more sheltered position under the warehouse. In casting off the stern ropes, someone also cast off the bow rope of the *Susanna* and she was blown out of the harbour. Captain Tom, after waiting until he was in a more favourable position, let go the anchors. They failed to hold. He managed to get sail on and tried to beat back into the harbour but in the face of the increasing gale, the *Susanna* was slowly being driven up the bay.

At last, with canvas blown to shreds, she ran on shore three-quarters of a mile to the south-east of the harbour where Butlins now have their holiday complex. The lifeboat stood to at five-thirty that morning and was launched at six. Luckily the crew was safe and no extensive damage was done to the forty-six-year-old vessel. The gale blew hard all the morning, moderating towards mid-day. In the late afternoon, the *Susanna* floated off, making the harbour at 4.30 pm. Twenty four hours later, she was on her way back to Porlock Weir to deliver her coal. 'Where've ee been? We thought ee was comin' in yesterday!' was the comment. No wonder even sturdy vessels like the *Penguin* here were lost at sea or wrecked on the rocky shores of North Devon and West Somerset.

37. Children posing within the dock at Porlock Weir

This family photograph was taken by Clifford Perkins in 1906 or 1907 and shows his friends and siblings posing for the camera. On the right of the picture is the smack *Samuel* lying over on her starboard bilge keel. These little smacks were built to lie on rough shingle beaches and often discharged their cargoes straight over the side, floating off as the tide rose. The *Samuel's* full lines can be appreciated as we see her underwater profile and her obvious depth in hold. She was built in 1860 down the coast at Padstow and was only 26 tons register. Before she was finally laid up here she was a regular trader to Lynmouth under the ownership of 'Farmer John'. It was sturdy little cargo carriers like this that were the mainstay of the rural coastal trade.

fig. 37

fig. 38

38. The French schooner La Mouette

This fine photograph was taken by Mr Alfred Vowles who started photographing in the locality during the first decade of this century. The earliest photograph in the author's collection is dated 1908. He became more prolific during the next three decades, often competing with Clement Kille in getting to incidents first. Alfred first worked from Porlock and signed his photos *Vowles Porlock* but from the mid 1920s he established a studio workshop in a large semi-detached house at the top of The Avenue in Minehead. His business flourished and he gained a reputation as a versatile newspaper and magazine photographer, in Exmoor and North Devon. Vowles certainly managed to get his photographic equipment to some pretty inaccessible places while following the hunt or taking shots like these of the schooner *La Mouette* ashore on Small Beach, a formidable place to get to on foot in February while carrying a tripod and plate camera.

On 12 February 1913 the fore and aft schooner *La Mouette* ran ashore on Small Beach to the east of Hurlstone Point in dense fog while bound from St Nazaire to Cardiff. She had been built in Dunkirk in 1869 by Anton Lefebvre and was always very well thought of. It was her intention to load coal at Cardiff and she was proceeding in ballast when she ran aground. Her captain was Josef Maheo of Paimpol. After the initial shock, the captain ordered two anchors to be put out over the stern in order to pull the vessel off and another tide gave him the opportunity. Meanwhile he sent two men to climb the cliff and make their way to the nearest town in order to order a tug. Both the captain and the crew were in high hopes of getting

her off during the next tide. The *West Somerset Free Press* on 22 February 1913 tells the dramatic story of what happened.

The French schooner *La Mouette* which ran ashore on Wednesday of last week has become a total wreck as a result of a heavy gale from the north-east. The vessel which is of about a hundred and seventy tons register, was bound from St Nazaire in Brittany to Cardiff for coal. The tides were falling last week, and a tug not being able to come at once to her assistance owing to the continued fog, it was soon realised that the vessel would have to lie there until Tuesday or Wednesday of the present week when the tides would have risen sufficiently to make it possible to attempt to float her. She would have remained comparatively safe had calm weather continued, which it did not. On Friday a tug was sent from Cardiff, but nothing could be done then, and after arranging for help to be given later, the tug returned, and the captain and crew remained by the vessel, sleeping on board each night...On the Monday the wind blew a gale from the north-east and sealed her doom, though the captain and crew did all that they could under the circumstances to prevent disaster. On Tuesday the tug appeared in sight, but the captain signalled to her that his vessel was too much damaged to float, and the tug returned to Cardiff.

La Mouette broke up completely in the heavy seas and all that remained of her a few months later was the rusting stem and keel which were jammed into the boulders of the beach. Much, however, was salved, some of it unofficially for as soon as the exhausted crew were forced to take refuge after the gale the locals went on board.

39. Porlock Weir men in the rigging

Porlock Weir men in the rigging of *La Mouette* after removing gear. One local said that, as a boy, he had crept on board while the crew were down below, and with a spanner had taken down the ship's bell and made off with it. He buried it in the side of the hill, not wishing to be caught with it until the whole business was long forgotten. Though he meant to unearth it, he was never able to do so for later he was called up for service in the Great War and there he lost a leg in action. After the war, though it took him all day, he returned to the spot but, try as hard as he could, it was not to be found.

However, as he remarked himself, 'When I was on board I could see other fellers on their way.' So it is entirely conceivable that the 'other fellers' saw him and dug it up themselves. Certainly bits of *La Mouette* were to be found in the cottages of local seafarers including her barometer proudly on view in someone's entrance hall. Her water tank lay for years just inside the dock at Porlock Weir.

40. Caerleon *and* Laureate *in the dock*

This is another of Clifford Perkins' pictures which shows two of his contemporaries posing with a model boat. It also shows the busy life of the dock in the first decade of the present century. The dock gates are shut; two vessels, a ketch and a smack, lie at the jetty and a second ketch is waiting in the main channel to load. In the centre of the picture is the ketch *Caerleon* and ahead of her is the *Laureate*. To the left of the picture there are the masts of other craft and probably the hull of the *Brunswick*. In the background you can see the premises owned by the Pollard brothers before it was converted to a dwelling.

41. *The ketch* Caerleon

Also by Clifford Perkins this shot shows the *Caerleon* after she was abandoned and committed to her last resting place well up the dock out of the way.

fig. 41

42. Inside the dock in the early 1890s

Here is the *Caerleon* again but in her working days. Ahead of her is the smack *Ranger* which was sold to Minehead in 1894 so this dates the photograph to the years immediately preceding this. In the left of the picture can be seen a vast pile of limestone waiting to be burned at the kiln behind and if you look carefully on the port side of the *Caerleon* you can see where the wall of the old quay had fallen into the harbour.

fig. 42

43. The dock in September 1912
&
44a and b. The clearing of the dock in 1913

By 1912 much of the dock was taken up with derelicts and it was decided to clear them all out and at the same time dredge out the entrance so that both trading vessels and pleasure craft could use it. At this time the dock was in demand by yacht owners from South Wales and it was envisaged that more visitors would use the facilities of the port if it was clear. So out of the dock came the *Sophia*, the *Caerleon*, the *RJW*, the *Herbert*, the *Samuel*, the *Betsy*, the *Brunswick* and the bones of a dozen rotting oyster fishing craft. The jetty was repaired and strengthened and room created to berth two vessels alongside the coal and brick wharf. New lock gates were fitted which promised to be more efficient than the old wooden ones which had been repaired several times. The work was completed by the summer of 1913 and the village celebrated with a regatta and an official entry to the dock with the squire present to cut the tape. Shown here on a brisk spring morning in 1913 are the tracks laid across the shingle and the steam crane brought by Messrs Johnson and Son from Bramley near Leeds. This crane provided power for removing hundreds of tons of shingle from the dock entrance and for levelling the berths within the dock.

fig. 43

fig. 44a

fig. 44b

45. The ketch **Dolphin** *entering the dock*

This picture by Clement Kille dates from the mid 1930s and was one of four taken on that day showing the *Dolphin* arriving, under tow, approaching and finally entering the dock. The *Dolphin*, like the *Emma Louise,* was one of the last regular traders to bring coal to the Weir.

46. The dock at Porlock Weir, September 1934

Railway carriages over thirty years ago bore photographs, usually four to a compartment, depicting resorts the length and breadth of the British Isles. British Railways (Western Region) negative no. B11169 survived complete with its date which is just what every photographic researcher needs. It is a quality shot taken on a large plate camera and extremely well composed. By the inter-war years trade involving sailing vessels had declined almost to a standstill. The *Emma Louise*, owned by Stan and Tom Rawle of Minehead, still visited as did the *Bessy Clarke* and the *Democrat* from over the Bar. A familiar sight in the Bristol Channel during the inter-war period was the wooden auxilliary screw ketch, *Democrat*, owned by Mr G. Clark of Braunton, a trim little craft, seventy one feet long, with a beam of nineteen feet and a seven foot depth in hold. She was built at Milford in 1909 by J. and W. Francis. Other visitors were mainly pleasure craft. A number of punts, skiffs, pulling boats and sailing craft were active alongside the visiting yachts and in these years it was easy to hire a pulling boat by the day or week from the Pugsleys or Leys. In the centre of the

fig. 45

picture is the Anchor Hotel, now grown to its full size with the addition of a second wing. A bus service was provided by Western National and Blue Motors. The inclusion of the bus in this photograph is significant for it indicates the growing importance of road transport over sea. Only twenty four years earlier Captain Wallis was bringing parties of visitors for day trips from Cardiff by a hired tug. Another coach firm worthy of note that brought visitors to Porlock Weir in the inter-war years was Scarlet Pimpernel Coaches of Minehead who ran a pristine fleet of immaculate vehicles, among them Leyland Lions and Tigers now so prized among enthusiasts.

To the right of the picture, the little coal jetty can still be seen and this is where the *Emma Louise* and the *Democrat* unloaded their cargoes of coal from South Wales and the Forest of Dean. On the left of the picture, just above the bows of the little carvel built boat, is the water tank from *La Mouette* still there in the fifties.

47. Porlock Weir in 1948

This picture, by Harvey Barton and Son of Bristol shows the ketch *Alfred and Arthur* unloading coal at the little coal wharf. Tied up ahead of the ketch is the Bristol Channel pilot cutter *Breeze* which, at the time of this photograph, was owned in Cardiff but based mainly at Porlock Weir. Of some 19 tons register, she was built in 1887 at Pill on the Avon below Bristol where many fine cutters were built. At the time of the photograph she needed repair and over the next five years she deteriorated rapidly. By 1954 the tide was coming up through the cabin floor. At this stage everything of any value had been stripped out of her and she looked a sorry sight. However, she was sold, patched and towed across the Channel for extensive repairs. Folk at Porlock Weir were delighted when she returned all spruced up with a new set of sails.

fig. 46

fig. 47

fig. 48

fig. 49

48. The pilot cutter Breeze alongside in 1984
&
49. The Breeze alongside in 1994

Breeze continued to be a feature of the port for many years, and we are indebted to her present owners for saving this one-time famous cutter. By 1996 she was again in need of repairs and was slipped at the Weir.

50. Porlock Weir village 1954

In the early fifties, most large national commercial photographers, including the Bristol firms, had stopped coming to West Somerset and stocks of postcards were becoming outdated. It was hard to find an up-to-date picture of Porlock or Minehead or one that did not show pre-war vehicles and fashions. After the war a lot of building took place and some of the older landmarks, like the Plume of Feathers Hotel at Minehead, were to vanish at the hands of developing vandals. Mr T. Blackmore of Bampton Street, Minehead, realised that there was no longer a local photographer taking local pictures and producing postcards. He gave up his business as a butcher, took over the old church hall in Bancks Street, bought an ancient hand-operated press and set out to produce a brand new series of postcard views of the entire area. He also took portraits. At the same time he started to make a collection of West Somerset photographs and, over a period of fifteen years, built up a marvellous collection, keeping a master set of copy negatives. The firm was extremely successful and Blackmore's postcards could be found in every possible outlet from Porlock Weir to Watchet. Eventually he retired and left Minehead, taking with him what must still be the finest collection of old West Somerset photographs in existence.

This picture taken by Mr Blackmore in the summer of 1954 shows the approach to the village and the cottages known as Gibraltar on the right. A brand new Standard Vanguard is parked outside the car park and there are one or two other modern vehicles in the shot. By the '50s Porlock Weir had shed its rural, agricultural and maritime interests in favour of becoming a pretty little tourist village with a picturesque harbour full of pleasure yachts. Only one or two youngsters decided on the sea as a career and it was no longer the case of sons following their fathers in the fishing industry for that, too, was in its death throes. So instead of focusing on shipping and trade, the photographer of the 1950s was intent on presenting a different image. Mr Blackmore consequently saw the cob cottages and the great banks of hydrangeas as typifying the village and did not visit the dock. The image had changed from that of a busy little working port to that of an attractive holiday resort.

51. Porlock Weir village 1956

Tom Blackmore, took this photograph a couple of years after the previous one. It shows Porlock Weir at an interesting stage of its development before the car park was made up on the site of the old fish market. One of Blue Motors Bedford coaches is parked at the bus stop. Blue Motors ran a regular service to Porlock Weir in competition with the Western National. A glance at the cars will reveal both pre-and post-war models with the modern ones standing out from the more boxy older styles. Austin, Ford, Vauxhall and Jowett are among the modern ones while in the centre of the picture is a lovely old drop-head coupe.

A study of the buildings shows the end cottage of the Turkey group before it was tastefully modernised and re-thatched. Also visible are two of the machine gun emplacements erected for coastal defence in 1939; the one on the right has since tilted and is beginning its slide into the sea. There is only one boat of any size left under local ownership, owned by the Leys, and this was used for herring fishing in season and for taking visitors for trips around the bay in the summer.

52. Hurlstone Point

Many names have been given to this prominent headland which marks the easterly boundary of Porlock Bay and the westerly extremity of the hill that rises to Selworthy Beacon. Orestone, Urdstone, Hurtstone and Hurlstone all emphasise the colour of the rocks that rise from the sea and contrast with the great sweep of pebbles that form the natural wall of the shore. Just to the west of the point is the Avon or Haven Pool where the Horner Water gathers behind the shingle before either filtering through or waiting for flood water to force its way through to the sea. The name 'haven' suggests that this was a place where vessels might have found a secure mooring in very early days and it would be interesting to investigate whether there are vestiges of a passage similar to the one that once created an entry into Dunster Haven some miles up the coast. It would coincide with the point of least resistance to the flooding river and therefore would have been formed and refilled with beach stones many times over.

Navigating the 'iron bound' coast of Exmoor has always been a hazardous undertaking and Porlock Bay was no place to be when the winds were from the north east making the whole stretch of shingle from Hurlstone Point to the Gore into a dangerous lee shore. Hundreds of vessels over the centuries have been blown ashore here. More dangerous was the stretch of high hog-back cliff that extends to Minehead past Hennerscombe or Annerscombe, Grixy, Minehead Bluff and Burgundy Combe. Blown ashore here the vessel would certainly be smashed to pieces giving the crew the option of staying put or making the difficult climb up the cliff.

On calm summer days there is nothing more enjoyable than a trip from Minehead to Porlock Weir passing close in under Hurlstone and perhaps between the point and the rock that appears at low tide just off the end of the land. However, before we sail on up the Channel let us drop back on the ebb and have a look at Lynmouth and its tiny ancient harbour.

fig. 50

fig. 51

fig. 52

Courtesy Dennis Corner, Porlock

LYNMOUTH

LYNMOUTH

fig. 53

53. The foreshore, Lynmouth c.1860

This very early photograph of Lynmouth was taken by Date of Watchet probably in the early 1860s. Lynmouth was chiefly a working river harbour. It has not altered much through the ages apart from the addition of breakwaters, groynes and eventually a harbour wall to prevent the blocking of the entrance by the prevailing westerly longshore drift. In Lynmouth's case the flow from the twin waters of the East and West Lyn rivers was sufficient to keep a navigable entrance clear for most of the year but occasionally winter storms on Exmoor would bring down debris and boulders which needed removal. Twice in recorded history massive damage was done involving considerable reconstruction work and the present retaining walls of the harbour are the result of rebuilding following the titanic storm of August 1952 which was of sufficient magnitude to warrant national attention and support. This storm co-incided with heavy seas and far exceeded the damage recorded when, early in the seventeenth century, cottages both here and at Porlock Weir were washed away.

Like Watchet before her present harbour was built, here is a huddle of artisan dwellings, workshops, fishermen's cottages, a working lime kiln and piles of imported limestone waiting to be dragged up the beach. There is very little that is pretty here. The only remarkable feature is perhaps General Rawden's tower which was perched on the end of the quay wall some fifty years before this photograph was taken. A story suggests that General Rawden used this edifice to provide himself with a sea water shower which was pumped up on a high tide and that it was built to resemble one of the navigation towers to be found on the River Rhine. In the photograph the tower forms the most seaward point of the harbour before the massive stone-built extension and timber pilings were put in place. Like other Exmoor ports the beach itself was used for serious fishing and traces of old weirs and ponds can still be seen. The dwellings here had little protection from the weather and

offered blank walls or very small timber-framed windows to seaward. In common with all the Exmoor ports the great fear was of the north-easterly gales, usually in the period December to February, when strong easterlies could set in for days and drive huge seas into the river mouth. Typical of these was the gale in January 1881 when the Bristol Channel Pilot Cutter *Cambria* was lost off Lynmouth. The *West Somerset Free Press* of 29 January 1881 reports:

Mr W. K. Riddell of Glen Lyn, Lynmouth writes....I am desirous to make known an act of bravery here in connection with the loss of the *Cambria* on Monday. John Union and John George Dibden, seamen on board the pilot boat *Cambria* of Newport, South Wales, had been engaged in putting their captain on board a steamer in the Bristol Channel, when the wind which had been blowing hard from the north east increased to a terrific hurricane. The result was that the whole of their canvas was carried away and the boat was rendered unmanageable. In this state they drifted about the Channel the whole of the dreadful night in a blinding snowstorm and under great personal privations, until about 10 o'clock the following morning, when finding that they were drifting on to the rock bound coast of Lynmouth without the possibility of escape, they were compelled to abandon the boat and take to the punt with the hope of saving their lives by running ashore between two high rocks under Ridiball. One of their oars breaking however, the punt became unmanageable and was swamped, and the men were thrown among the breakers. Dibden managed to save himself, but Union had twice been swept back by the receding waves, and the third time, having become exhausted, he would have most certainly been drowned, had not Phillip Burgess, master of the *Nautilus*, of Lynmouth plunged into the foaming surf and succeeded in rescuing him.

Captain Phillip Burgess worked out of Lynmouth in a variety of vessels and enjoyed a reputation as a splendid seaman used to action rather than delegation. The above was typical for on another occasion when on board the *Conservator* he leapt overboard with a line to rescue a seaman who had fallen from the shrouds in appalling weather off the Foreland. *Nautilus* was the second vessel of that name to be owned in Lynmouth: the first was registered under the ownership of John Crowcombe in 1805 and sold on in 1835.

A last look at the photograph shows mooring posts in the foreground which were still in use sixty years later

54. Two smacks rigged for unloading c. 1865

Here two largish smacks are lying up the harbour and the inboard one is unloading coal. The gear can be seen plainly as baskets of one and a quarter hundredweight are winched out of the hold on a hook and carried ashore along the plank into a waiting cart. In the 1860s three men or often two men and a boy discharged in a day which was a regular backbreaking task but part of the routine of serving in coastal sail.

At this time, the sturdy smack was the maid of all work in the smaller ports and these two would be typical. Almost all were tiller steered, even the big ones and all carried huge areas of mains'l which needed skill and strength in handling. The inboard vessel here displays the beamy characteristics of the early century and would be massively built to withstand constant use on shingle beaches.

This photograph was taken some years before the lifeboat house, reading rooms and major guest houses were built to crowd the little streets. The lifeboat station was founded in 1869 and was to remain until 1944. Harbour traffic was never sufficient to warrant the removal of buildings as in Quay Street, Minehead and consequently it was only storm damage that diminished the little town.

55. The smack **Conservator** rigged for unloading below the slip c. 1885

This is Captain Phillip Burgess' vessel *Conservator* preparing to unload in her own port in the mid-eighties. The *Conservator*

was built in Padstow in 1843 and like many of her contemporaries was later rerigged as a ketch. Sadly she was lost in January 1890 on a voyage from Cardiff to Lynmouth with a cargo of coal. She was in collision with the barque *Concezione* and sank shortly afterwards. This photograph shows the main slipway used for all the commercial traffic and almost all the picturesque cottages so often photographed since. In the centre is The Rising Sun which, like The Ship at Porlock Weir had been an inn for centuries.

fig. 56

56. The ketches Lily and Stucley

Difficult to date exactly, this picture clearly shows the added stone groyne and timber pilings extending from the end of the harbour. Added to prevent the inroad of beach stones into the harbour mouth, it also protected the little tidal landing below the slip where vessels could lie up in safety. The *Lily* of Barnstaple was a regular visitor to the port. The *Stucley* has just run in under headsails and mizzen and will take her turn to unload. The *Stucley* was never quite sure how her name was spelled and on one occasion someone painted *Stuckley* across her stern, leaving the original spelling on her bows. She was registered as the *Stucley* but traded for several years with both names in evidence. Spelling was an art that few rustic sailormen mastered and they would go to great lengths to avoid having to admit that they couldn't spell.

57. The Three Sisters and the Melbourne

Here we have the ketch *Three Sisters* of Cowes, owned as we have previously discovered, by Captain Tom Ley of Porlock Weir. She was built in 1800 at Plymouth as a smack but like so many others ended her career as a ketch. Modifying and converting vessels was a skill that all local shipbuilders and boatbuilders could turn their hands to. There are photographs of the Pollard brothers of Porlock Weir at work on quite large vessels showing that even the smallest ports possessed the skills necessary to support a lively coastal trade. Whilst this was the case in the nineteenth century Captain Stan Rawle later remarked that there were few left who could rebuild the rudder trunking on his ketch *Emma Louise* in the late 1940s as all the old lads who possessed these skills were fast fading away. Alongside is the little smack *Melbourne* of Bristol, built at St Ives in 1865 as a three-masted lugger and owned in 1905 in nearby Combe Martin. By 1910 she was owned by Captain Richard Ridler who ran her with his son Jack mainly between Bristol and the Exmoor ports.

fig. 57

fig. 58

58. *Two ketches lying up in Lynmouth harbour c. 1910*

A splendid picture from British Railways showing two worka-day ketches rigged for cargo handling over the side. The round sterned vessel is the *Eleanor Mary* of Bideford, built at Milford in 1865 as a schooner so is found here with a considerably reduced but more easily handled sail plan. Originally owned in Milford by Captain Phillip McCarthy she was sold to Captain E. J. Pedder of Lynmouth who was her owner when this pho-tograph was taken.

59. *The ketch* Lily *lying in Lynmouth harbour*

The ketch *Lily* of Barnstaple secured within the harbour about 1916. The *Lily* was built in Penryn, Cornwall in 1897 and was brought to Lynmouth from Topsham in Devon via Ilfracombe. In Lynmouth she was owned from 1916 to 1927 by Alfred Oxenham. She was not lost until January 1929 when it is recorded that she foundered off the River Usk. The *Lily* held

just six 10-ton trucks of coal which was the ideal cargo for small yards like Lynmouth. There is a lovely description of a voyage in the *Lily* from the Newport River to Lynmouth by Edmund Eglington who published his life in these little coasters in a book called *The Last of the Sailing Coasters*. Published by H. M. S. O. in 1982 it is a must for all sailing craft enthusiasts. Like the *Emma Louise* at Minehead, she carries the distinction of being the last sailing coaster to be owned at Lynmouth. Worthy of note is the number of wooden pulling boats on the river bank. There are thirteen here and probably more out of shot. They are an indi-cation of the growing importance of the holiday trade and the demand for hire boats. At this time both sea and river fishing was a prominent feature of the little port warranting a special mention in all the local guide books. Sea fishing was carried out mainly from October to April by long line and hand line. Mr Cecil Bevan held the record locally and in 1908 took 675 pounds on his long line off Lynmouth. He also boasted a record for conger, well known along this coast for size and always afforded a healthy respect. His biggest, caught in 1907, weighed 56 pounds. Not only was fishing from open boats by line popular but also by rod and line and by hand line from the shore where

fig. 59

in the summer months good bass were taken along with pollack, grey mullet and whiting. There is also evidence that weir fishing was popular in the early years of the twentieth century where whitebait was commonly found. Fishing the foreshore by weir, pool, nets and gullies was long established all along the coast and papers leasing foreshore rights can be found in local archives back as far as the fourteenth century. Herring fishing was the preserve of the locals and always kept apart from the fishing of a sporting nature. Between October and Christmas, larger well-found boats would drop down on the ebb to *shut* their nets returning on the flood hopefully with a good haul. However, apart from sporadic good results, the legendary harvests of the seventeenth and early eighteenth centuries have never been repeated.

60. Vessels in Lynmouth harbour c. 1910

This photograph was obtained from British Railways in the early sixties and shows a ketch, a smack and a sailing boat. The smack, probably Welsh built, is carrying her rudder 'out of doors,' much like the little *M & E* of Minehead and is similarly constructed. This is the *Melbourne* of Bristol and she has almost certainly brought domestic provisions down from the city for local shopkeepers. The ketch is the *Little Jane* which was owned in 1893 by John Crowcombe of Lynmouth. I am grateful to Terry Belt of Winchester, a keen marine historian, for identifying these two craft by the indistinct lettering on their sterns. In the case of the ketch, only *ANE* was clear and in the case of the smack, only *RNE* was distinguishable. The *Little*

Mouth of the Lyn Lynmouth. W2320.

Jane was built in 1858 at Porth in Cornwall as a smack. and after passing into the ownership of John Crowcombe, stayed at Lynmouth until the end of October 1910 when she was wrecked at Clovelly.

In the foreground is a pretty little sailing boat probably belonging to Mr Bevan who had been a very keen fisherman and whose wife was the proprietress of the Lyn Valley Hotel. In 1910 this boat could be hired at 3/- an hour or 20/- a day which was quite expensive when you could stay at the Lyndale Hotel for 2/6d a night or enjoy a double room for 4/- with breakfast at 2/6d, lunch 2/6d, tea for 1/- and dinner for 4/6d.

61. One of Campbell's paddle steamers collects passengers at Lynmouth

A wet August afternoon in the late 1890s and a fleet of local boats are ferrying passengers out to join one of Messrs P. and A. Campbell's White Funnel Fleet for a trip to Minehead, Weston super Mare, Barry or Cardiff. The steamer would lie off Lynmouth and passengers would be ferried to and fro in open boats. The steamer is likely to be on the return leg from

Ilfracombe picking up the passengers she dropped earlier after their 'run' ashore. The smack in the picture is the *Mary* of Barnstaple. She is rigged for unloading and the pile of limestone in the left foreground is likely to have come from her hold. She is also flying what is probably her full locker of flags and this suggests that the steamer's visit might have coincided with a local regatta.

62. The **Little Jane** *and the* **Samuel**

I was very pleased to find this photograph of the smack *Samuel* as the only other one I have discovered shows her as a wreck lying within the dock at Porlock Weir. This picture shows her as she was when she was still working.

63. *Lynmouth harbour c. 1896*

This photograph shows two new features; the building at the top of the slipway and the splendid cliff railway known as the lift. The lift was introduced to the town by Sir George Newnes, a prominent local benefactor, and building went on through 1889 with the official opening taking place in 1890. Just over nine hundred feet long, the track rises behind the little harbour facilitating the carrying of freight as well as the expected passengers. In the early days, with the passenger accommodation removed, bulky cargo was often carried up and even the occasional heavy motor car was lifted in this way to avoid the perilous ascent by grit and pebble trackways. The ketch *Nautilus* has arrived on the tide together with three local sailing boats and they are all drying their sails.

fig. 62

fig. 63

This photograph is almost certainly by Graystone Bird of Bath who provided photographs for the range of illustrated guide books like Ward Lock and Company at the beginning of the twentieth century.

64. *The smack* May *unloading timber*

Another grand photograph from British Railways taken with a full plate camera. The smack *May* is busy unloading timber over the side into a waiting cart while the horse stands patiently up to his knees in the river. If you look beneath the stern you can see that a cargo of limestone is being carted up the slip to the nearby kiln. The *May* was built at Chepstow in 1817 and registered at Bideford. Here, she is well on the way to reaching her century an age that many local vessels achieved with ease.

It is marvellous that so many craft survived for so long. They must have been incredibly strong or patched and rebuilt over and over again following each near brush with disaster which of course happened regularly. Looking very much like the *May* the smack *Molly* was built here in 1759. Of 29 tons, she was owned by the Crowcombe family. Another Lynmouth smack was the *Betsy* built here in 1773 and owned by William Lock. She was lost in 1803 on the Irish coast with a cargo of oak bark on board.

fig. 64

fig. 65

65. Lynmouth harbour c.1912

This photograph bears all the hallmarks of Messrs E. A. Sweetman and Sons of Tunbridge Wells whose aim was to produce an atmospheric seascape rather than a concise narrative photograph. The focus is the vessels but it is not easy to identify them. The picture also shows dozens of wooden boats lining the river mouth but the accent is on composition rather than detail appealing to the romantic and obviously attractive to the thousands of visiotrs who bought this postcard over the years.

66. The Lynmouth lifeboat in Porlock Bay 1936

This is a shot of the Lynmouth boat taken by Clement Kille as she left Porlock Weir on the return leg of a practice launch in 1936.

fig. 66

MINEHEAD

MINEHEAD

fig. 67

67. Minehead Harbour c. 1720

This is the earliest extant painting of the port of Minehead and used to hang at Dunster Castle.

There is little doubt that it commemorated the building of the new Quay Head which, coming as it did in an era of commercial prosperity, enhanced an already busy harbour and allowed Minehead to remain a key port for the import of wool from Ireland which was admitted into only a few nominated west coast ports bringing both revenue and profit into the town.

In the reign of Elizabeth I the townspeople successfully petitioned for a charter and for control of their port. This was granted. However poor management and an inability to make contingency plans soon saw the existing harbour in ruins. The Luttrell family of Dunster Castle, Lords of the Manor, had the available finances to rebuild and this they did on a site to the westward where the foundations of the present harbour were laid. The ensuing quay served the town well throughout the seventeenth century until the enlargement, pictured here, made the port even bigger. In the ledgers of the time the new work was termed 'The New Quay' and it allowed more ships to berth and be unloaded on each tide.

The painting, probably by an itinerant landscape painter, shows a crowded Quay Street with houses on both sides of the road and it is possible to identify some of the field patterns, especially Yard Acre, which continued until the 1880s. The church tower and the cottages of Higher Town can be seen as can the pinnacle on the top of the church tower which was finally removed in 1764 when it became unsafe. Ossy Point to the west of the harbour is shown and also Greenaleigh beyond. Immediately behind the harbour a vessel can be seen under construction in Manston's Yard where craft were built until the end of the eighteenth century. Both coastal sloops and deep sea square-riggers are depicted and local hobblers can be seen at work securing the vessels to the post in the centre of the harbour. The square-riggers are brigs typical of the traders that could be found in the Atlantic and Mediterranean trade throughout the eighteenth century.

68. Minehead harbour in 1735

Painted by George Wood on paper primarily to emphasise the newly enlarged harbour, this 'prospect' is also interesting as it points out local landmarks as well as Middle Town, Lower Town and of course, the Key. High on the summit of the hill

fig. 68

is marked a place called Compass, a visible spot from which vessels could take their bearings. Another point, called White Mark, just around the headland indicated the anchorage.

Minehead's history as a port has fluctuated as markedly as the tides that rise and fall in the Bristol Channel. Periods of ruin have been followed by periods of remarkable growth and they in turn have been followed by further decline. In its glory Minehead traded with the West Indies and America, with the Mediterranean ports and with Ireland. Throughout the seventeenth century, Minehead owned and traded some of the largest ships afloat and played an important part in the sea drama of the nation often warranting mention in the State Papers. Trade boomed and it was not until the little port was eclipsed by the larger commercial centres on the Bristol Channel and the size and capacity of vessels outstripped her facilities reducing her from an international port to a coastal one that it lost its big port status and settled for what it could get. Despite this, Minehead became a valuable local coastal exchange of domestic industry with links to all major centres. Most of the pictures that follow show a busy harbour with a lively coastal trade.

fig. 69

69. Minehead harbour 1825

This little pen sketch appeared in a neat booklet produced by William Dunne. It contained several aspects of Minehead which might appeal to persons of fashion for by now visitors were travelling to this region for its climate, sea bathing, walking, riding and later hunting. The popular impact of the Romantic Movement in both art and literature meant that a steady flow of appreciative gentlefolk were seeking suitable lodgings from where they could follow in the footsteps of Wordsworth and Coleridge and at the same time hire a bathing machine on Minehead sands for their health. Minehead, with its proximity to Lynmouth, Porlock and the newly-appreciated 'romantic' expanses of the Brendon Hills and Exmoor early discovered that it could attract tourists. By 1830 regular coach services were established to both Bridgwater and Taunton and visitors were staying in the popular Plume of Feathers Hotel in the centre of town as well as in rows of 'genteel lodging houses'. From the beginning Minehead set out to become a better class of resort and many of the lodging houses were adapted for a superior client to those found in the more crowded resorts.

70. Minehead harbour 1827

This small pencil sketch is dated 1827 and shows the cluster of buildings that surrounded the harbour most of which can be

fig. 70

identified in photographs taken in the 1860s although only one or two still exist. This competent little drawing also shows how bald, rough and stark the hill was before the arrival of the fir plantations. Only two trading sloops are shown and the absence of cargo on the quay waiting to be loaded gives an impression of inactivity which would not often have been the case. There are no fishing boats shown or any trace of the large gallows crane which should appear in the centre of the drawing so it should be remembered that, although accurate in some respects, this is a romantic impression and consequently suffers from artistic licence.

The early decades of the nineteenth century saw a slow decline from the impetus given in the previous century, and although the figures from the 1813 survey of the port of Minehead seem healthy enough, averaging as they did 211 shipments over the years 1810-1812, the position was far from encouraging. Savage, writing in 1830, gives only six vessels as belonging to the port, two in the Bristol trade and the rest trading to Wales. By far the largest number of cargoes loaded were outward bound at this time. Kelp was shipped in large quantities from Watchet and Minehead to Bristol in the 1790s where it was used in the glass industry and grain, flour, malt, hides, leather, timber, bark and, in season, 'chemical wood', were steady imports. 'Chemical wood' was the term given locally to green oak, cut in early May from the scrub oak of the Exmoor coast. Culbone and Embelle woods were impor-

tant areas to the industry, which in the early years of the nineteenth century employed twenty to thirty men. The wood was cut and stripped of its bark, then shipped to Bristol and Swansea where methyl alcohol was obtained by destructive distillation. The return trips were made with domestic and manufactured goods, provisions and beer. Whilst on the subject of beer, there is the lovely story of the Minehead vessel returning from Bristol with casks of beer on board. Feeling thirsty, and unable to enter Minehead due to an ebb tide, the crew bored a small hole in one of the casks... When the vessel had not come in on the succeeding tide and remained, swinging at anchor in the bay, Minehead folk became anxious, not so much for their fellows as for the cargo. The vessel was towed in.

71. Minehead Bay 1860

Taken in 1860 by James Date of Watchet from the top of the North Field, this is probably the earliest photograph of Minehead Bay. Down below is Captain Vickery's ivy-clad cottage, later demolished to widen Quay Street, and Lamb Cottage on Lamb Corner, once a school for small boys kept by a Miss Brazier at sixpence a day. If you look carefully on the seaward side of Captain Vickery's cottage you can see that he owned a considerable stone groyne which was joined to a substantial wall at the side of the property. You can just make out

fig. 71

his personal bit of beach where it would be possible to bring a boat in but not to secure one permanently as this area is very open to the sea. Nestling into the hill opposite Captain Vickery's cottage is the old thatched Red Lion Inn whilst on the right of the picture is Mr Ridler's sawmills still known today as Ridler's Yard.

The Bratton Water runs uncovered where the Avenue is now and apart from a couple of barns since demolished there is no other development to be seen. A footpath links the outfall of the Bratton Water along the top of the shingle ridge towards Lamb Corner and Quay Street. A slight depression on the landward side of the shingle bank can still be seen, indicative of the earlier weir land form but soon to be filled and covered forever with the construction of the road and pavements adjoining the new sea wall. The three trees standing by the outflow of the Bratton Water survived all the development and remained for another hundred years. Trees in photographs are often useful in establishing the position of vanished buildings or in measuring the passage of time by their height and girth.

A large smack is unloading limestone in the bay and you can just make out the horse and cart which will haul the stone to the kilns at the bottom of the North Field. Although obviously not as sheltered here as within the harbour, this site was a traditional one for running in and unloading cargoes on the gently shelving beach.

72. The Beach at Minehead in 1874

This is another fine photograph by James Date of Watchet taken straight off a plate glass negative. It shows the undevel-oped foreshore destined to become the Esplanade. The picture was taken at a point where the Esplanade now joins Warren Road, then a sandy lane linking the town with Warren House way out on the marshes and once a centre for fowling and, during the Napoleonic Wars, a lookout station.

The unsophisticated nature of the beach can be appreciated as can a lack of people using it but the bathing machine shows that this part of the beach was in use for sea bathing. Upon payment of one shilling, due to the Lord of the Manor, a horse would draw the machine into the water and the intrepid bather, suitably clad, would emerge timorously into the muddy waters. The beach hereabouts remained under the ownership of the Lutrells of Dunster Castle and so a toll was extracted for all traffic passing the tollbar and a charge made for the use of the beach. This was an ancient right which was established in feudal times when the Lord of Dunster Castle held the foreshore rights for the full extent of the port of Minehead, a rare honour as the foreshore rights usually belonged to the Crown.

A large smack hull lies across the site of the present road. The sea defences consist of large pilings driven into the ground and backed with timber and beach stones. There are also a couple of prominent groynes, the nearest being timber-built. The Esplanade Buildings can be seen nearing completion and awaiting window frames but the new engine shed at Minehead Station is in use. Thomas Lloyd, staying at Number Four, The Esplanade, Minehead in August 1898 found himself staying in a 'most attractive gentleman's residence' and the Handbook to Minehead published in 1895 at 6d speaks of The Esplanade as a large block of buildings intended principally as lodging houses 'the land and marine views from the upper rooms being most enchanting'.

fig. 72

fig. 73

73. North Hill, 1874

This photograph by James Date was taken on the shingle at low tide from the bottom of the present Avenue. It clearly shows the hill before the first houses were erected and the ancient hedge pattern was broken up; only St Michael's Church and Shute Farm are visible. The North Field, The Ball, and Weir Field or Ware Field are clearly defined as large arable enclosures like Weir Cleeve, Yard Acre, Quay Meadow and Perkins Field. Several of these were to give their names to roads. Contemporary sources successively name the hill itself as Weir Hill, Compass Hill, Beacon Hill and North Hill, each name deriving from a function or local geographical feature. The name Weir Hill, possibly the earliest, describes the hill as overlooking the large weir harbour at its foot. The name Compass Hill refers to the time when the high ground above the harbour was used for navigational bearings. The name Beacon Hill, still preserved in Beacon Road and the Beaconwood Hotel, derives from the time when warning fires were constructed on high ground to raise the alarm in case of invasion. North Hill, the name that became established on the first Ordnance Survey maps has remained as the definitive title, rising as it does above the medieval North Field. The name Minehead itself describes this hill headland and is close to the old English word that means hill. Perhaps most significant of all is the proximity of Quay Meadow to the old quays that lined the weir harbour rising as it did from behind the courtyard of the old Red Lion and opposite what is now the widest part of Quay Street.

The whitewashed property, Lamb Cottage on Lamb Corner, stands out prominently as does the thatched and ivy clad cottage belonging to Captain Vickery. Half a dozen piles of limestone lie in the bay.

74. Lamb Corner 1870

Nothing in this photograph by James Date remains today except the hill itself. Lamb Corner, with Lamb Cottage, marked the beginning of Quay Town and stood enclosed within its own sea wall. At this time a very irregular sea wall extended from Lamb Corner to the Quay. It was nothing like the present one and existed for much of its length as individually maintained back garden and outhouse walls to the cottages that backed on to the beach. The cottage is Captain

fig. 74

Vickery's property, one of the buildings erected in the mid seventeenth century on the site of the abandoned weir wharves when the port was enjoying a period of prosperity. These cottages, like the old Custom House that was demolished in 1900, are not as old as the cottages on the landward side of the road. The gabled and thatched building in the centre of the picture is the Red Lion which was one of the oldest inns in the town.

The wreckage of a wooden boat and the baulks of timber in the foreground mark the top of the Haven beach where timber and limestone cargoes came ashore. Today the line of the new sea wall crosses the centre of this picture, all the cottages on the seaward side of Quay Street having been demolished to accomodate the widening of the access road to the harbour. The last indication of the buildings that once stood along this stretch of shore was cleared away in the early 1920s when the area was levelled and grassed over.

Lamb Corner owed its name to a disaster that took place on 22 February 1735 when the Bristol transport *Lamb* was wrecked with a heavy loss of life. The story started on the morning of 20 February 1735 when a company and a half of Colonel Hargreaves' regiment enshipped with their families from Bristol to Ireland in order to strengthen the garrison there. The *Lamb* was a nearly new vessel, built in Bristol and under the command of Captain Morgan. The company under the command of Captains Frankford and Williamson set sail shortly after eleven o'clock. As they entered the Channel they were assured of a quiet, uneventful voyage. However by the evening of the 22nd, 78 people including both officers, had perished in a great storm which had risen from the north east.

The vessel was blown ashore at Minehead, where she quickly broke up in mountainous seas. The following day, 35 men, women and children were buried in one grave in Minehead churchyard; the rest were interred in the nearby churchyard of Dunster.

75. Quay Street circa 1885

There are several photographs taken from this viewpoint a little way up the Church Path and it is possible to see how over the years the gradual destruction of the buildings and gardens on the seaward side of Quay Street took place. Although the major part of the demolition took place in the early 1920s when the roadside cottages were pulled down, some of the barns and garden walls were removed in the early 1880s in order to make way for George Fownes Luttrell's Sea Walk which enabled visitors to walk on a firm path all the way from the harbour to the Esplanade. The sea wall then followed this path which established the present layout.

76. The continuation of Quay Street circa 1875

This print from a plate glass negative of 1875 shows what sort of damage can occur if the plates are not stored carefully. This is another of James Date's photographs and is part of a photographic essay which started in the bay and, after following the line of Quay Street, ended in the harbour itself on a day when

it was crammed with wind-bound vessels. Some of Minehead's oldest houses are in Quay Street with their origins in the fifteenth century. The larger two-storey houses date mostly from the early seventeenth century and were built at the same time that the new harbour was constructed. In the gaps which today form small gardens and courtyards there can be found the foundations of former buildings and there are the remains of cellars and outhouses built into the hill itself behind this row. Written records in leases and wills provide evidence that what we see today is only a vestige of the extent of Quay Street in the eighteenth century.

77. *Quay Town circa 1868*

This is an enlargement from a plate glass negative taken by James Date around 1868 and is one of the earliest that shows Quay Town in its entirety. From Captain Vickery's little beach along the entire length of the street to the crowded huddle of cottages at the head of the slipway can be seen the dwellings of sea captains, mates and seamen. Quay Town had a character all its own and the landsman was treated with some suspicion. In social terms the quayside dwellers saw themselves as a breed apart, having little in common with their country cousins from 'out over'.

A further look at this photograph will reveal, apart from the scratches and dust of a century or more, wooden stakes set in the sea, evidence that fishing the foreshore was still a healthy occupation in the 1870s. From the historical point of view, the sites of Lynmouth, Porlock Weir, Minehead and Watchet, whilst being quite different in character, offered from necessity regional centres for a developing fishing industry both offshore and inshore. All offered sizeable inshore fishing opportunities for the longshoreman. All the sites then were equipped with complex systems of weirs, pools, gulleys and stakes to obtain the maximum harvest at every tide. There is an exciting body of evidence to support the fact that quite a considerable industry was developed from early times on the foreshore between high and low water springs. The foreshore fishing rights at Minehead included all the foreshore between Bugundy Chapel to the west and Bradley Gate (Blue Anchor) to the east. Documents relating to these fishing rights are found as early as 1299 and there is a wealth of references to be found during the ensuing centuries. A fishing weir was a low stone built wall of massive construction set with stakes and woven with wattles like a hedge. They were nearly always in the form of an angle with the apex inclined towards the withdrawing tideline. Often built in two rows, one for the neap and one for the spring tides, they required constant maintenance. This form of fishing was very popular from the thirteenth century and remained so in the described form until well into the seventeenth century when the introduction of nets instead of wattles became more common. A typical document from the Dunster Castle Muniments describes how in March 1455, one Thomas Chapman leased a cottage and a garden at Minehead with 'lez stackes in mari'. Even in the mid-twentieth century the method was still in use although galvanised iron pipes were used on the traditional sites instead of wooden stakes. The popularity of establishing ponds and pools extended from Norman times and perhaps even earlier as the Saxon inhabitants would not have been unaware of the benefits of fishing without boats. Their latterly diminishing acreages are recorded splendidly on successive Ordnance maps and their names have only just been forgotten. Greenaleigh Pool, a genuine weir pool, is now smaller than at any previous time, Crab Pool has vanished and Owl Pool gradually disappeared some thirty years ago. Big Weir, Old Man's Weir, Martin's Weir, Brazier's Gulley, Iron Gun, are mostly forgotten. The Madbrain Sands have been preserved for us through the courtesy of the Ordnance Survey.

fig. 77

fig. 78

78. The Harbour from the beach, circa 1875

Another classic from James Date showing Minehead harbour and the buildings around the slipway. In the early seventeenth century large herring shoals made their way into the Bristol Channel. From this time forward until their eventual disappearance, the fortunes of the coast were assured. At Porlock Weir and Lynmouth, as well as at Minehead, Red Herring Houses began to appear for the purpose of drying the fish. They were called red herrings because after salting and thorough smoking they assumed a red colour and it was in this form that they were exported all over the country. At Porlock and Minehead, hostels were opened to cater for tradesmen coming to buy the fish.

For nearly two hundred years this abundant supply continued and then, within a five year period, the herring became more difficult to catch. In the last years of the eighteenth century as local trade began to diminish, so did the fortunes of local fishermen and the number of craft began to fall. The larger ones converted to cargo carrying and there are records of Minehead fishing boats at Bristol and Bridgwater with hides and bark. As the number of fishing boats declined, the focus altered from the small regional and specialised ports to larger centres where specific vessel types had developed to fish the major off-shore fishing grounds. It was the larger craft with more modern equipment operating out of ports of national importance and with good lines of communication to the major centres of population that took the lion's share. Minehead's fleet ceased to have any real commercial importance.

From late Victorian times the occasional good herring season along the Exmoor coast was the exception rather than the rule and as such warranted a mention in the *West Somerset Free Press*. The season of 1895 was one such. 'Minehead herrings were uncommonly plentiful this season, local fishermen having some very large takes. The largest quantity taken by any one boat was six maze or thirty hundred. These big catches caused the price of herrings to drop and at one time herrings were being hawked in the town at two shillings a hundred.'

After the Great War herring became scarce again and the fleets dwindled to a handful of motor boats during the 1930s. In company with Harold Bushen, Jimmy Heard and the Slades, Stan Rawle fished on in season for a while but more than often the catches hardly paid for the petrol. In 1947, hopes were raised briefly when catches of about a thousand a tide were taken but it was short lived. Today it is fishing for sport that boats are kept for and it is the visitors that charter them.

79a. The harbour at Minehead circa 1875

The quality of this photograph by James Date in terms of contemporary detail, clarity and condition is outstanding. Of the buildings, only one remains and that so altered that you might miss it if you didn't know where to look. The Chemical Works on Quay West can be seen in the distance.

Prominent in the shot is the large 'gallows' crane, known locally as Griff's Gallows after Captain Griff Pulsford who was over zealous for its maintenance and predated the Health and Safety Executive by a century. A steam crane didn't arrive on the quay until 1887 and this one, identical to those working in the middle ages, was the maid of all work and the local lads were happy handling it despite the effort required. In the centre of the picture is the building that was the Customs House for the harbour from the time when this harbour was built. Built on three floors, the ground floor was the main office and all the harbour notices were posted in the window and on a board just inside the door. Shortly after the building of the Pier Hotel in the late nineties and the construction of the pier in 1900, this interesting historical building was demolished and its function removed to premises along Quay Street.

79b. Detail from the previous picture

In this enlargement the Customs House is seen more clearly. In building style it is close to the building erected at about the same time at the end of the row known as Gibraltar at Porlock Weir. The buildings to the right at the rear are in poor shape and did not survive the century. The fishing boats in the foreground show that despite the obvious decline in the local industry several quite large boats fished on as registered craft.

Stan Rawle gave the following little rhyme which he said was current when he was a lad to enable the youngsters of the port to remember some of the names of local fishing boats.

> Lively, Lion, and the Lark,
> Tom Bowline and the Shark,
> The Why Not and the Bucky Blue,
> Who'd a' Thought It, What Say You.

The nearest pictorial record of these local square-sterned fishing smacks is found here in James Date's work in the seventies. Here we can see two active Bridgwater registered vessels lying under the harbour wall in the traditional berth between the two quays.

fig. 79b

fig. 80

80. Square and round-sterned sloops in Minehead harbour circa 1875

Taken on the same day as the previous shot this Date photograph shows a line of wind-bound smacks secured within Minehead harbour. The two outboard ones have kedge anchors out as they are too far from the mooring post but four are secured to the post. Here is the little French built *Eugenie*, the *Queen* of Cardiff, a Gloucester vessel and the *Henry* leaving two vessels unidentified among these typical nineteenth century rural smacks, all home built and familiar in these small country ports. Rugged little vessels, they would take almost anything anywhere and often found themselves up obscure creeks, on remote beaches or, like here, wind-bound in a Bristol Channel port unable to proceed – a most frustrating business as it inconvenienced owners, masters, merchants, consignees and crew who often went hungry when all the victuals ran out and there was no money to buy more.

Still afloat in the 1870s and indeed at the turn of the century were sloops that were built in the 1790s and it is easy to recognise them by their hull form with their 'apple bows', broad beam and accentuated sheer. They would sit on the water 'like a broody hen' as one skipper remarked. These craft would have been built in tiny town yards, on exposed beaches and on improvised slips on riverbanks. In rural nineteenth-century Exmoor the skills were there to do a tidy job of building vessels just as they were there for building carts and wagons inland. The rigging, blocks and iron work were locally made in ropewalks, workshops and smithies close at hand which meant that individual ideas were developed and local idiosyncrasies proven in practice. Ideas like roller reefing for a speedy reaction to adverse conditions were developed and patented in several places and seamen had strong opinions as to which stood up the best in a stiff blow.

81. The same craft on the same day

This is an enlargement showing the same line of vessels taken by James Date on the same day as the previous photograph some dozen paces further along the harbour. This was a timed exposure indicated by the movement of the vessels' sails.

fig. 81

fig. 82

82. A bird's eye view of Minehead harbour from the same series

This view taken by Date from the hill overlooks the area behind the harbour which consisted for the most part of a tumbledown collection of workshops, boatsheds, old dilapidated cottages that would be swept away before the end of the century. This area formed the nucleus of commercial offices and merchants' premises that serviced the quay following its building in the second decade of the seventeenth century and most of what you can see here is from that date. The slight depression in the shingle and the track marks the site of the launching slip of what was Manston's Yard. Vessels were built here for centuries and in the painting we looked at earlier there is a vessel on the slip here. The last vessel to be built here of which we have a record was the *Unanimity* built by Thomas Manston in 1798. She was a typical country sloop similar to the ones illustrated in the photograph. A Certificate of British Registry shows that on 2 August 1803 James Crockford was her owner and John Bushin her Master. She was certified as having one deck, one mast and a length of 38 feet. Her beam was 14 feet 8 inches and her depth in hold was measured at 7

feet 4 inches. She admeasured 33 tons and was described as a square-sterned sloop duly registered at the port of Minehead. Earlier documentation reveals that she was built for John Fownes Luttrell at a cost of £160.10s. 9¾ d. and her first Certificate of Registry was made out at Minehead on 28 July 1798.

83. The cottages on Quay West circa 1868

This smaller negative by James Date was found in the album of photographs that were kept by the family and which was passed on to his grand-daughter Mrs Lyddon. It was wrongly titled by Date himself, proving that even the photographer could make mistakes. He put the caption 'Watchet' underneath and it is certainly true that this shot is similar to a view across Market Street towards the West Pier with the older part of the harbour opening out beyond the London Inn. However there is no doubt that it is a rare view of the cottages in Quay West looking towards the rear of the Old Customs House. The reason that folk could be puzzled today by this picture is that nothing remains of these old buildings as they were swept away

fig. 83

when the Pier Hotel was built, the gas works extended and the Lifeboat House arrived. This picture also offers evidence that there were dwellings on the landward side of the road before the gas works were extended and the gasometers erected.

84. The harbour at Minehead 1880

There are three smacks here together with half a dozen fishing boats. The smack lying in the middle of the harbour is Thomas Kent Ridler's *John and William* which was built at Porlock Weir back in the summer of 1858 and launched into the little dock there. She was built by Thomas' father John in partnership with Captain Will Pulsford who was registered as her owner. She remained a familiar sight trading out of the West Somerset ports until she was tragically lost on Barry beach when she failed to get off after loading limestone for Minehead. Like so many of her contemporaries the *John and William* was converted to a ketch and a later photograph shows her rigged this way. The nearer smack is the *Jane and Susan* which enjoyed the reputation of being the fastest craft operating out of Minehead. In June 1861 she broke all existing speed records by making the trip from Minehead to Bristol in four hours and forty eight minutes without the aid of steam up the River Avon. In the background can be seen the pre-1900 profile of old buildings including the Customs House and the old original slipway before the inner end of the harbour was rounded off and cased in with a neat stone wall.

fig. 84

85. Minehead harbour 1888

This commercially produced sepia flimsy of 1888 shows how quickly development took place throughout the eighties. In 1887, Thomas Kent Ridler built his coal cellar on the quay, a building that has since become a landmark itself and now houses comfortable flats. The same year, the steam crane arrived enabling coal cargoes to be discharged into large iron buckets rather than into baskets which had to be manhandled ashore along a plank. In the right of the picture can be seen the infant gas works of the Minehead Gas Light and Coke Company and the manager's house built on Quay West in 1868. Above on the hill the newly excavated road with its railings is visible and above that again the new conifer plantations are beginning to rise above the scrub and heather cover. In harbour opposite the Customs House is the smack *Sophia* with coal from Penarth. Old John Ridler, the founder of a considerable local business in timber, stone and coal died in 1876 and passed on his business and maritime interests to his son Thomas who further developed them and went on to become Minehead's last significant vessel owner. In all he owned half a dozen sturdy craft beside a trim yacht which he sailed from the harbour.

fig. 85

fig. 86

86. The Customs House, Minehead 1892

This photograph is one of the local classics from the studio of Herbert Henry Hole of Watchet, Williton and Minehead. The founder of the firm was Herbert Henry (Bert) who was born in 1836 at Watchet. His son, Walter Groves Hole, was born in 1880 and continued with the business following the death of his father in 1900. In turn, his son, Herbert Henry, carried on the business from Long Street, Williton until his retirement in the 1970s when the family collection of negatives was sold to Michael Bouquet, a keen collector of nautical photographs. Bert Hole was an adventurous photogra-

pher with an inquisitive nature who made a comprehensive collection of plates about the full range of local activities.

It was Bert who took this famous shot of three of the vessels belonging to Thomas Kent Ridler in Minehead harbour. The left half of this full plate negative is reproduced here showing the ketch *Argo* and the smack *John and William.* The *Argo* was launched in Swansea in the July of 1868 financed by T.K.'s father John and Captain Henry Pulsford. Like other craft owned or built by John, they were all to end up in the ownership of T.K. as he came to be called on the quay. In the early eighties the *Argo* was converted from a smack to a ketch and it

fig. 87

is in this rig that she is seen here. Two years following this photograph, both these vessels were to leave Minehead, the *Argo* being sold to Appledore in 1894 and the *John and William* to be wrecked on Barry beach the same year.

87. The tops'l schooner **Perriton**, *Minehead harbour 1892*

This is a photograph of the last vessel to be built at Minehead. She was commissioned by T.K. and built just below his sawmills and woodyard high on the Haven Beach by Ben Williams of Watchet. Williams had also worked on the *Argo* for T.K.'s father and his work was held in high regard locally. A man of many skills, he had the eye of a craftsman and the experience of a well travelled seaman having worked around the world in sail as a ship's carpenter and spent some years in Australian and American shipyards. Together with the *Star of the West* which he helped to build in his native Watchet, the *Perriton* was to be his swansong. Lacking capital to build 'on spec', he left the area and went to work at the Royal Albert Dock and later Tilbury Docks where he was successful as a shipwright. In his retirement he lived in South Wales and often sailed the eleven miles across the Channel to Watchet or Minehead in a 28 footer. He died in 1931 when in his nineties having seen the final demise of local merchant sail within his lifetime.

The *Perriton*, named after the hamlet where John Ridler had his farm, was T.K.'s flagship when it was launched in March 1881 and a huge crowd gathered to watch the event. The *Perriton* remained a familiar sight locally and can be spotted in several photographs of the harbour over the next few years. Captain Thomas Chidgey painted her several times. She did not have a happy end as during the First World War she was stopped by a U boat and sunk by gunfire in 1918.

The picture also includes a view of T.K.'s coal warehouse and the steam crane which arrived in 1887. The photograph was a timed exposure as evidenced by the swinging bucket dangling on the hook. The men have been very good and kept still! It's a pity that we cannot catch a glimpse of Captain Joe Webber, the last skipper of the *Perriton* who thought he was being lazy when he finally gave up the sea at the age of eighty two. Stan Rawle used to tell of the marvellous characters there were on the quay when he was a boy and looked up to them for their skills, their intrepid personalities and obstinate determination to ovecome all that nature could throw at them. He spoke of Jack (Bunnel) Slade, Jimmy (Guckoo) Morgan and Billy (Fairy Cakes) Burnett and many other seamen and longshoremen with outstanding reputations for bravery, tenacity and humour. Nicknames were indicative of the close-knit communities where trust and humour went hand in hand with the daily struggle of surviving in the face of daunting odds. Watchet too had its characters and

fig. 88

they are remembered by names such as Margarine Jack, Billy Go Deeper, Old Bottles, Shackles and Hopping Jack.

88. Seamen standing on the quay at Minehead, 1892

Taken on the same day as the previous shot, this general view of Minehead harbour includes some seamen that Bert Hole persuaded to pose for him. In shot is the tops'l schooner *Perriton* and the smack *John and William*. The vessel with the painted ports is the *Bessie Clarke*. The seaman's dress is typical of their working gear with rough serge or heavy canvas trousers and a blue gansey, or in today's parlance, guernsey. Each seaport had its own distinctive pattern often with the name of the owner knitted into the bottom. Should a sailor be washed ashore it would be possible to identify his port of origin and often his name. Many were knitted all of a piece on a number of needles and were works of art in their own right. The headgear is interesting as it shows both the seaman's peaked cap and the bowler hat which predated the use of the flat cap in universal use among the coasting fraternity in Edwardian times.

There is a notice painted over the doorway of the gabled building to the left of the Custom's House. which says 'The Sailors' Home' and was an initiative of Mr Luttrell's when he tried to wean the local seafaring community off alcohol which was being consumed in enormous quantities in Quay Street

public houses. The Sailors' Home was a coffee shop and probably a very good one but it failed to attract the sort of numbers that Mr Luttrell was hoping for and after a few months it reverted to a store.

89. The sloop Looe, circa 1880

This is one of Frith's earlier photographs and shows the eighteenth-century sloop *Looe* in Minehead harbour about 1880. She was the oldest member of T.K.'s fleet, built at Looe in Cornwall in 1787 and not owned at Minehead until 1876 when T.K. took a shine to her. Like many other sloops she was heavy to handle and to make life easier she was converted to a ketch although in this rig she never looked right. This was the craft that 'sat on the water like a broody hen', a reference to the design of her bows which were blunt and lacked the flare and run that was to appear in the late eighties and nineties. Another description of these ancient vessels was 'apple-bowed' which, with a pronounced sheer, gave them a 'cocky' upright seat in the water. Despite her age, the *Looe* did well enough for T.K. in her role of stone, timber and coal carrier up and down the Bristol Channel but mainly to Porlock Weir and Minehead with coal and limestone. She was loading limestone at East Quantoxhead in 1905 when she strained badly and failed to get off on the tide. Despite throwing out the cargo too much damage had been done and it was felt that she was not worth the extensive work needed. She was patched up temporarily

fig. 89

and broken at Minehead the same year with much of her gear going to other craft in the fleet. Nevertheless at 118 years she had done splendidly, a tribute to the country craftsmen who had built her.

90. Minehead, 1890

By the time this engraving was done, Minehead was fully on the map as a holiday destination. This panoramic view by John Swain was probably commissioned for Cox's popular guide which sold throughout the nineties and was descriptive of the region's villages, walks, flora and fauna. The artist has included every possible facet of the town's appeal to the visitor. From left to right there is the railway station with its link via Taunton to the rest of the country. Then there is the newly constructed Sea Walk upon which the visitor could now stroll from one end of the bay to the other. Next, the bathing beach with its machines and the expanse of sand extending from the new beach breakwater and then the hotels which are easily identifiable as the Beach Hotel and the Metropole Hotel. In between them is the Esplanade Building which together with the Beach Hotel formed the bottom of Station Road which was renamed The Avenue. On the hill is Clanville and Elgin Towers, built in 1887, the precursors of dozens of other Victorian and Edwardian residences and hotels that were built on this superb

fig. 91

fig. 90

site. Sailing is also highlighted as is the steamer leaving the harbour for Wales or for other coastal destinations. The surrounding hills and Bratton Ball, Hopcott and Dunkery Hill are featured amongst a great sweep of countryside behind the town.

91. The Launch of the George Leicester, 1902

This photograph, taken from the new pier shows the launch of Minehead's first official lifeboat from the newly constructed lifeboat house in 1902. In the left of the picture can be seen the rear wing of the Pier Hotel and the white gabled building that had acted as the house for the rescue boat that had been stationed here before the arrival of the RNLI boat. Behind the lifeboat house, which has recently been extended, is the rear view of the row of cottages that once lined the seaward side of Quay West.

The picture shows just how large the crowd was that came to witness this event and you can be sure that the numbers packed on to the pier would be as great. This was quite an event and long looked for as in the days of sailing and pulling boats, a delay of half an hour could, and often did mean the difference between life and death especially in winter and the nearest boat down Channel was at Lynmouth whilst the next one up Channel was at Watchet. This Exmoor section of the Bristol Channel was long notorious as an 'iron bound' coast and vessels caught in the many severe north-easterly gales found it well nigh impossible to claw off when driven over from anchorages on the other

side of the Channel. Equally, north-westerly gales have been the cause of several wrecks between Lynmouth and Minehead.

The George Leicester was a self-righting sailing and pulling boat and was to do sterling service at Minehead until replaced by a second boat of similar design called the Hopwood in 1927. The last pulling lifeboat stationed at Minehead was the Arthur Lionel which arrived in 1931. The motor lifeboat, the Kate Greatorex, did not arrive until 1939. A further look at this picture shows that one of the launching crew, whose job it was to handle the heavy wooden skids with rope handles, has just fallen flat on his face as the weight of the boat passing has flipped the skid over before he could let go. Two other men are just releasing a skid and one of them can be seen immediately behind the coxwain. The practice of launching a boat on skids down a steeply shelving beach was an old one and widely used by lifeboats in other parts of the country. However there was a problem for both Minehead and Watchet boats when the tide was a long way out and then the boat was taken on a carriage out into the sea by horses and later by tractor. The site of the lifeboat house here is on the traditional launching site where vessels were built from the seventeenth century. The last real lifeboat to be stationed at Minehead was the BHMH named from the initials of the family that provided the legacy enabling her to be built. She arrived in 1952 and was withdrawn from Minehead in May 1973 after inflatables had amply demonstrated that they could cope with all local conditions and situations.

fig. 92

92. The building of the pier in 1900

This photograph used to hang in the back room of the Pier Hotel just adjacent to the 'penny in the slot' automatic piano that so many generations had poured beer into that it sounded nothing like a piano. There were probably a lot more taken of the construction of the pier as it was to become a very important asset to Minehead and there had been talk of one for ten years. The plans for the proposed pier in the Somerset County Record Office in Taunton show that drawings were prepared in 1894 together with plans for reducing the size of the harbour adjacent to the Pier Hotel by building a new semi-circular wall against which a new slipway would replace the one that had served the old quay since 1616. All these developments were to be completed by 1901.

93. The pier in 1901

This is one of W. G. Hole's photographs of the pier at Minehead shortly after it was opened on 25 May 1901. At 250 yards long it provided a permanent deep water jetty for visiting steamers at all states of the tide there being two levels, one to cope with low tides and the other with high, a system still in use at Ilfracombe. The pier was an immediate success and Minehead became a more popular excursion destination than before. Even before the construction of a pier at Minehead, steamers brought day trippers from Barry, Cardiff and Bristol often unloading as many as 1500 on high days and holidays.

The *West Somerset Free Press* for 7 July 1894 notes that 'one thousand five hundred passengers disembarked from Wales' and we can be sure that they patronised the Pier Hotel and the Red Lion on their way into the town. There were the inevitable grumbles from the more sober residents but the additional income was welcome and there were no complaints from the shopkeepers and innkeepers.

Barry Railway Company's Red Funnel Fleet and the White Funnel Fleet of Messrs P. and A. Campbell could be seen most days and regular timetables were published to effect communication between Minehead and Lynmouth, Ilfracombe, Barry, Penarth and Cardiff. Day trips could be arranged to Tenby, Mumbles and Lundy Island, and trippers could be assured of every comfort on board. These wonderful old steamers with their great thrashing paddles, gleaming machinery and scrubbed decks were run like yachts by lads from every seaport on the Bristol Channel. Some signed up for the season only whilst others were happy to serve in them for years. One or two more elderly seamen, having retired from the rougher life of chucking limestone in and out of ketches were quite content to work on a day-to-day basis, returning to port at the end of the working day with no night watches. Campbells were very ambitious in those early days and worked hard to see off the opposition, so it was not long before they had a monopoly in the Bristol Channel. Based up the River Avon in Bristol, they would set out at the break of day and after a regular programme of plying to and fro from Weston-super-Mare to Cardiff to Minehead to Ilfracombe to Minehead to

Cardiff to Weston-super-Mare, they returned to secure and clean up for another day.

As their name might indicate, Messrs Campbells originated on the Clyde where the original Campbell brothers owned and chartered paddle steamers. One of the best known was the *Waverley* which was chartered by a syndicate of Bristol businessmen in 1887 to examine the possibilities in the Bristol Channel. The season was so successful that Campbells themselves decided to expand into the area and in 1893 the whole enterprise became a limited company which went from strength to strength and continued to expand around the coast to take in the major ports and holiday resorts of the south coast. When the First War arrived they owned 13 steamers most of which were to be drafted into war work as minesweepers. The biggest was the *Brighton Queen* and the newest was the *Glen Usk*. After the war, refitted and repainted, they resumed their peacetime role and continued to ply the Bristol Channel to all the established ports. By the outbreak of the Second World War, Campbells had no rivals but neither did they enjoy the vast numbers of passengers that had bought tickets before the First War.

fig. 94

shelters built on it as a response to passengers' complaints that 250 yards exposed to the full force of whatever was blowing at the time was sufficient to soak them or blow them inside out before they could reach the shelter of the Pier Hotel.

94. Minehead pier, 1914

This shot, taken by Kille from the foreshore, shows one of Campbells steamers, probably the *Ravenswood*, disembarking passengers. You will notice that the pier now has two

95. Minehead pier from the top of the gasometer

Another shot by Kille when he hit on the idea that there might be a good view of the pier from the top of the nearest gasometer.

fig. 95

96. Minehead pier from North Hill 1938

This is the pier as many remember it, looking down from the road at the top of the Zig Zag. Minehead would have a pier now had not misfortune struck in May 1940. In common with every seaside resort in the country at the outset of hostilities in 1939 preparations were made to resist the invasion that everyone expected Hitler to initiate within the year.

Thousands of posts were driven into the beach between high and low water and concrete pyramids were erected on all the slipways. Pill boxes were built along the shoreline and concrete machine gun emplacements hastily thrown up and disguised as buildings with shingle roofs. The harbour was declared out of bounds as was the pier and a wooden barrier laced with barbed wire was placed across the entrance. Minehead harbour was used as a gun platform and an ancient weapon of First War vintage was mounted on a concrete base and disguised with the outline of a house or harbour building. The gunners quickly reported that they could not traverse the gun effectively because the pier was in the way and when this observation was finally passed up to the War Office an order was dispatched to dismantle the pier and take the resulting scrap to Newport. The job was completed by May 1940 by which time there had been further observations from the gunners that they feared that the recoil and detonation were affecting the foundations and that in their estimation the platform was not sufficiently strong. By the time that this had filtered through to the War Office department responsible for local coastal defence, it had become clear that Hitler's proposed invasion of the United Kingdom was no longer at the top of his list and an order was posted to remove the gun.

fig. 96

fig. 97

No steamers called at Minehead until some years after the war when Campbells decided to survey Minehead harbour to see whether it was feasible to bring the steamers into the harbour as they used to do before the pier was built. During the war and for a number of years afterwards a huge pile of shingle had accumulated at the harbour mouth which meant that vessels using the harbour, like the *Mary Stewart,* had to negotiate this awkward barrier and were limited to entry at high tide. This veritable mountain was finally removed in the early fifties and the way was open for the steamers to visit once more. There was considerable excitement in the town when Campbells announced the day and the time of the first post-war visit of one of their steamers. They didn't say which one and there was great speculation as to which vessel it would be. The hour approached and a smudge of smoke was seen on the horizon. The steamer came nearer and nearer and proved to have a single funnel. Finally she swept across the bay broadside on to the onlookers on the sea front – a wonderful picture. The telegraph rang, she reduced speed and slid into the harbour with ease. She was the *Ravenswood*.

From the fifties to the seventies Campbells continued in the Bristol Channel and destinations like Lundy Island via Ilfracombe were as popular as ever. However, the number of passengers consistently declined and Campbells finally stopped running trips from Minehead in 1979. They ran a single season in 1980 for the Landmark Trust but after that the White Funnel Fleet called no more at Minehead. There will be those who lament the passing of *Cambria, Ravenswood, Glen Usk, Cardiff Queen, Bristol Queen,* and the *Britannia* whose pounding paddles and pristine pistons will never be experienced again. Screw steamers are not the same.

97. Minehead harbour, 1898

This well-known photograph from the Frith stable shows the old slipway shortly before its removal and the old extent of the harbour which was very close to the front of the recently erected Pier Hotel and did not leave sufficient room for traffic to pass easily. At the top of the slipway can be seen the roof of Pulsford's weighbridge office which was also destined for removal. This is the last photograph of the Custom House and the adjacent thatched and gabled building on the other side of the little yard. They were all to go except for one building that could not be demolished because it had been left to the town for all time and a curse placed upon anyone who should interfere with it or the revenue it produced for the poor of the town. The building in question was a warehouse or cellar on two floors and you can see it squeezed up against the wall of the Pier Hotel. Over the years, it was periodically refurbished and rebuilt and in this picture you can see that it has recently had a new roof and a new sliding door to the ground floor entry. Before this it was thatched.

This remarkable building was put up at the same time as the harbour itself and is contemporary with some of the cottages at this end of Quay Street. Only a few of the interior original features remain and, as it was extensively rebuilt in Victorian times, there is little to tell of its age. In the seventeenth century it was owned by the Quirke family, a prominent merchant and seafaring family of some stature and importance in the town. The story goes that Robert Quirke, caught at sea in a wicked gale, promised certain charitable works should he be allowed to reach his home port again. He did so, and was as good as his word, building, in 1630, a row of almshouses for the poor of the town and giving the proceeds of his quay cellars for their upkeep. Legend has it that the alms houses were built from ship's timbers and that the ship's bell was hung at the end of the row. However there is no truth in this romantic tale as an examination of the timbers has proved that they were cut for the job in hand and a ladder up to the bell proved that it was a gift from Robert's son fifty years after the alms houses were built to commemorate his father's generosity. The bell is dated and signed and is therefore far more valuable to the town than

a seventeenth century ship's bell. The brass plate, crudely cut, that records the gift of the almshouses and the cellars to the town is still in situ on the row of cottages. It records the gift and the curse which has helped to preserve this quayside building from falling down. Curses were taken very seriously in those days and perhaps they still are.

On the other side of the Pier Hotel under the hill is another building that was to be demolished by 1900. This was the New Inn, built at the same time as the harbour.

98. Minehead harbour, 1900

On the death of Herbert Henry Hole in January 1900, his son Walter Groves Hole took over the business. He was twenty years old and every bit as keen as his father to maintain and further the business. As the years went by he was to expand the photography business and open a studio and gallery in the centre of Minehead as well as at Williton. He expanded his father's range of cards and views and was keen to take as many newsworthy pictures as he could. In the summer of 1900, he started to take a further selection of local and general views to update the stock of available post-cards and prints for sale to the visitors. This picture and the one following were a part of this update. In the first we can see the ketch *Standard* on the left. In the background is the little 19 ton smack *Harriet Ann*

fig. 98

fig. 99

which used to fetch coal for the gasworks from the South Wales ports and on the right, awaiting her turn to unload, is the ketch *Destiny*. The *Harriet Ann* was built at Swansea in 1856 and was owned at the turn of the century by the Webbers of Minehead. The *Standard* was destroyed in the titanic gale that smashed Watchet harbour in December the same year, just months after the taking of this photograph. She was built in Fowey in 1837 as a sloop and like many of her contemporaries was later altered to a ketch. When this picture was taken, she was owned by Alfred Nicholls of Watchet. In the background can be seen the newly constructed semi-circular wall and slipway that fronted the Pier Hotel. They were built in 1900. The *Destiny* of Bridgwater was run by Griff Pulsford who bought her from Falmouth a few years earlier. She was built in Jersey in 1867 as a 'dandy' or 'dandy-smack'. This was the name given in some quarters to the early development from a sloop or smack rig to that of a ketch where the main boom was shortened and a pole mizzen stepped to ease handling.

99. Minehead harbour, 1900

This picture was taken within a few minutes of the previous one. The *Destiny* is preparing to unload and a hand is setting up the cargo gaff. You can see him standing on the inboard end. Under the quay just out of shot is a little smack unloading bags of flour to Harry Baker's dray drawn by his patient horse Prince. A bearded, three badge Coastguard rating is also

posing for the shot. In the background, the Pier Hotel is complete and the only building that remains of the previous centuries is Quirke's building which, protected by a local charity, could not be demolished. The New Inn is still there in this shot but destined to be removed because the road was very narrow there and traffic to the gas works increasing.

100. Children at Minehead harbour, 1902

Sometimes a family album yields treasure indeed and this wonderful photograph belonged to Miss Wills who lived almost opposite the quay all her life. She is present in the picture and recollected the day when it was taken. An added bonus is the fact that she had the names of all present. From left to right are Bill James, Tom Heard, Rose Wills carrying Jack Wills, Lucille Martin, Jack Martin, Dolly Burnett, Elizabeth Martin, Harry Wills, Jackie Wills, Ted Collins (behind) and Harry Chapman who was sadly lost in Minehead's last Regatta.

101. Minehead harbour, 1908
&
102. The Orestes alongside the coal cellar, 1906

Of all the old quayside buildings in previous photographs only Quirke's cellars remain and by the time this picture was taken,

fig. 100

fig. 101

fig. 102

the ground floor had been turned into a little chapel dedicated to St Peter and known as St Peter's on the Quay. The room above was tidied, refurbished, given some windows and turned into a reading room for the population of Quay Town. These alterations were felt to lie within the spirit of the original gift and were completed in 1907. The new semi-circular wall to the harbour fronting the Pier Hotel can now be seen as can the new slipway.

The main vessel in the pictures is T. K. Ridler's *Orestes,* his favourite. Mostly she was skippered by Captain Thomas (Hammer) Rawle and very well looked after by him until the vessel was finally sold to a Mr Stead who wanted it for a private yacht. Also in the first picture is T.K.'s own yacht *Triton* a gaff rigged cutter with a running bowsprit. She also had a comfortable cabin which enabled T.K. to go for lengthy trips which he often did with Thomas Rawle at the helm.

fig. 103

103. Fishing boats in Minehead harbour, 1908

By the end of the First World War, all these craft had vanished and were replaced with open 30-footers that could double as passenger boats for the holiday season. Fishing was no longer a profitable business and certainly could not support the construction or maintenance of vessels of this type. The boats in the photograph represent the last type of fishing boat specifically designed for local conditions. Between 30 and 40 feet long, they were half decked with broad beams and narrow sterns. Endowed with plenty of sheer they were rigged as cutters with a topmast and a running bowsprit and looked to be handy vessels in the often steep seas that could be experienced off the Exmoor coast. The two largest, including the *BR80*, are almost as big as the trading smacks behind them and are registered professional craft, although by the time this picture was taken they must have been experiencing lean times.

104. Minehead harbour, 1908

Another shot of T.K.'s yacht *Triton* lying in the harbour.

fig. 104

105. Minehead harbour, 1909

In the centre of the picture is a Bristol Channel Pilot Cutter. Two ketches are secured behind and the bows of the *Triton* can be seen in the left of the picture.

106. Minehead harbour, Winter 1910

There is certainly nothing romantic about this picture, snapped by Kille in the November of 1910. You can just make out the form of the *Thistle* and the *Susannah* but the identification of

fig. 105

fig. 106

any other craft is difficult. T.K.'s yacht is in its usual berth and is easily identified by its white painted cabin. The picture is unusual in that it was taken out of season and is not the more popular sunny, warm or attractive view.

107a and b. The Great Gale of 1910

Heavy seas in the Bristol Channel can quickly become mountainous in nature and extremely destructive. The 1910 gale smashed up the Sea Walk, the shelters, the beach defences and most of the existing promenade. A glance at the *West Somerset*

fig. 107a

fig. 107b

Free Press records quickly yields the dates of the major gales since the 1860s as each was memorable in what it destroyed locally.

108. Minehead harbour, September 1912

This is a much clearer shot by Kille taken at the end of the summer of 1912. The *Triton* we recognise in the left of the picture. Behind her is J. B. Marley's graceful *Thistle* skippered usually by Captain Jack Bell of Watchet. Astern of her is the *Orestes*, built by Banks of Plymouth in 1885 and in the right of the picture is the ketch *Susannah*, built at Appledore in 1860. Both lie at the quay head having crept in on the tail end of the tide. The *Orestes,* T.K.'s favourite, was a particularly good looking vessel of some 57 tons. She was brought to Minehead in 1896 and was still trading out of Minehead throughout the twenties. Never again would the harbour see as many sailing vessels in port at the same time. By the thirties, only one local vessel remained and visiting sailing craft were so rare that they were worth going down to look at.

109. The back of the harbour, 1912

This snap also came from Clement Kille, and shows one of Minehead's more eccentric figures, Sam Can, whose real name was James Slade. Sam Can was the nick-name of the character on the right who lived in an old wooden boat hauled high and dry on the shingle behind the harbour. The uniformed man

fig. 108

fig. 109

fig. 110

with the telescope is a Coastguard rating whilst the man in the centre is a Mr James who was a bit of a local historian and collector of folklore.

110. Minehead harbour, circa 1913

A number of ketches crowd into Minehead just before the First World War. Ahead of the *Maggie Annie* is the *Orestes*. By the end of the war many vessels had been lost and others had been thrust out of the commercial market by the increase in road and rail traffic. This was the end of the coaster with the exception of those that landed local contracts to established firms needing a regular supply of raw materials.

111. The Orestes *about to unload coal c. 1920*

T.K.'s *Orestes,* heavily laden with coal, is waiting to be unloaded alongside his coal cellar. On the right we can see a lorry with solid tyres waiting for the first load where the patient horse used to stand in pre-war days. In the centre of the picture is a bus with its driver posing alongside. This was the traditional starting point for all bus journeys leaving Minehead and long after the pier was demolished and the harbour ceased to have any passenger potential, both Western National and Blue Motors continued to start their journeys here. In the distance there is a gap where the New Inn used to stand before increased traffic required its demolition.

fig. 111

fig. 112

112. A ketch alongside c.1919

A workaday sailing coaster alongside the quay snapped at Minehead by Clement Kille shortly after the First World War. Some seamen, dressed for shore-going in their flat caps, jerseys and coats are obviously posing on board for the camera. The seaman in the centre of the picture is probably the skipper and he's still in his working gear. If you look carefully you can see that the gaff is rigged for cargo handling.

113. The **Thistle** *alongside in Minehead harbour*

This pretty ketch is J.B. Marley's *Thistle*, registered at Faversham and owned by him for his brick and tile business in Minehead. The *Thistle* was contemporary with the *Orestes* and the *Susannah* and could often be seen in company with these vessels in the harbour. She was built in Plymouth in 1887 by Watson and Fox and was a familiar sight around the coast. There is a record of her at Minehead in 1904 under the ownership of John Marley. It is thought that she was lost in the English Channel just before the war.

fig. 113

114. Clement Kille's picture of the Orestes

There is no way of knowing when this study was made although it is probably from the mid 1920s as the *Orestes* was sold in 1929 and never returned to the West Somerset coast. She was bought by a man called Stead who fitted her out for an expedition to the Cocos Islands which meant of course that he was after treasure. Nothing much else is known about the subsequent history of this fine vessel except to say that the rest of her career was as a private yacht and that at a later stage she had painted ports. She met her end in Tanga Harbour in 1955 having struck a beacon and sunk.

fig. 114

fig. 115

115. Captain Tom (Hammer) Rawle

Captain Rawle in conversation with John Slade on the quay at Minehead in the summer of 1919.

116. The **Emma Louise** *in Porlock Weir dock*

The *Emma Louise* seen filling up the jetty at the Weir was the last sailing vessel to be owned at Minehead. She was built at Barnstaple by the famous yard of W. Westacott in 1883. She was a vessel of 72 tons and measured 75 feet with a beam of 19 feet. During her days at Minehead she regularly brought coal to Minehead and Porlock Weir from the River Severn ports of Lydney and Sharpness, from Newport, Port Talbot, Swansea and from the Eley River. An occasional cargo of coal came from Saundersfoot, as early as the eighteenth century.

fig. 116

fig. 117

117. *The* Emma Louise *about to load pit props, 1932.*

In 1932 the *Emma Louise* was a prominent local feature of Minehead and a regular visitor to Porlock Weir. At this late stage she still carried a full suit of sails and is seen here with her topmast and jib boom which inevitably were shed when she became little more than a motorised coaster during the second World War. She was owned by Captain Stan Rawle whose father had skippered the *Orestes*. Stan and his brother Tom sailed and worked her together and like their father before them, maintained the very high standards of seamanship that became the hallmark of the family. When the *Emma Louise* finally left Minehead in the mid-fifties she brought to an end

ship-owning in West Somerset being the last sailing vessel to be owned in the town.

118. *Tom and Stan Rawle bring the* Emma Louise *home for the first time.*

The importance of obtaining valuable primary evidence is nowhere more obvious than in searching among family records where some remarkable finds are made. This actual snapshot was carried around in Captain Stan Rawle's wallet for decades as its condition denotes. It depicts the occasion when the brothers Tom (left) and Stan brought the *Emma Louise* into

fig. 118

Minehead in September 1926 after purchasing her and marked the beginning of a partnership that was to last until there was no more trade left to support the venture and the *Emma Louise* needed extensive, expensive repairs. She finally left Minehead in 1953. Between them they represented the last of a seafaring tradition that went back to the beginnings of local history. Both were magnificent seamen.

119. *Quay Street in the early 1920s*

This photograph comes from the Minehead Council archives and shows work in progress to widen and raise the level of the road to the harbour. These alterations swept away the houses, gardens and outbuildings that were sited on the seaward side of the road and replaced them with a lawned area and a shelter

fig. 119

for visitors. The road level was raised several feet at this point necessitating a retaining wall being built alongside the cottages which is there to this day. One of the reasons for this was to attempt to prevent the flooding that took place regularly on spring tides. However, the flooding continued and even today the cottagers are prudent to take the necessary precautions when extremely high tides are forecast.

120. A mantlepiece at Quay Street, Minehead

This picture is from the Hole studios and depicts a much carved mantlepiece in a cottage at Quay Street.

121. Captain Smith of Minehead

This is a lovely shot of Captain Smith who, legend has it, was the character upon which Players Cigarettes based their advertising campaign for Navy Cut. His face was, thereafter, destined to be displayed upon every packet of Players the world over. There are probably many claims to this honour but certainly the story of Captain Smith's portrait has been circulating in Minehead for decades. Here he is walking along the sea wall with a young lad who was destined to become a Lieutenant Commander in the Royal Navy. Perhaps the model yacht tucked under the Captain's arm had something to do with it!

fig. 120

fig. 121

fig. 122

fig. 123

fig. 124

122. The Orestes *and a steamer in Minehead harbour, 1927*

The *Orestes* is lying outboard of the steamer *Wheatsheaf* which has berthed alongside the quay and is taking up most of the room.

123. Captain Smith at the quay head, 1928

A steamer has nosed in at the quay head. *Orestes* is in the background and Clement Kille has asked Captain Smith to pose for him.

124. *A steamer entering Minehead harbour, 1928*

Hobblers are assisting a steamer to enter the harbour watched by the crew of the *Orestes* and a crowd on the Quay. The photograph is by Clement Kille.

125. *Motor fishing boats at the quay 1928*

In the foreground Jim Martin's boat has just come into the harbour. Jim Slade's boat is behind. These boats are not designed as fishing boats but fished for herring in season with about a dozen nets. In the summer they carried visitors on regular trips around the bay. Clement Kille took this picture. The vessel in the background is the *Orestes*.

fig. 125

fig. 126

fig. 127

126. The three masted schooner Mary Jones in Minehead harbour, 1929

Visits of the larger extant schooners were rare and when they did call in at Minehead they were worth a photograph. Clement Kille snapped this one lying up in the harbour for a few days in the summer of 1929. She was owned at the time by Captain Billie Shaw, the brother of Captain Hugh Shaw who owned the *Cambourne*. Both brothers were exceptional seamen and kept on in the coastal trade with sailing vessels until it was impossible to carry on any longer. The *Mary Jones* was finally lost on the Goodwin Sands in the winter of 1932. When this picture was taken she was fitted with an engine which necessitated taking down her tops'l yards. However Captain Billie fitted her with a light squares'l yard about 25 feet long and often set a large squares'l to assist the engine. You could recognise her by this and by her high bow and Atlantic sheer for she was once engaged in the Newfoundland trade.

127. A jury-rigged fishing boat at the quay head, 1926

Jim Martin's boat is here rigged with a gaff mainsail, a foresail and an improvised mizzen with which he can save fuel as he fishes off Minehead. There were no purpose-built fishing boats left at Minehead when this picture was taken and it was a case of going out with whatever was available. In the left of the picture is the hull of the *Orestes*.

fig. 128

fig. 129

128. A Clement Kille study of the Orestes, 1926

129. The three masted schooner Cambourne in Minehead harbour

Another schooner that visited Minehead in the twenties was Captain Hugh Shaw's *Cambourne*. The *Cambourne* was owned outright by Captain Hugh who developed a successful business at a time when many other coasters were giving up. He did this by sheer tenacity and determination and by cutting his freights to the bone whilst delivering cargoes to places where others would hardly dare. He survived some terrific gales and on one occasion was blown out into the Atlantic with his bulwarks washed away and most of his canvas torn to shreds. The sea was

in his blood and he was a very fine seaman. In this picture can be seen the *Orestes* and the *Emma Louise*. This photograph was another of Clement Kille's romantic pictures like the previous shot (fig.128) of the *Orestes*.

130. Wooden sailing and pulling boats at the quay head, 1930

What a joy it is to catch a glimpse of these beautifully made boats. It is satisfying to see that the love of wood has prevailed and at last we are beginning to see some splendid boats built again. We owe this shot to Clement Kille.

fig. 130

131. Minehead harbour, September 1933

This photograph is from British Railway's archive. Jim Slade is in his boat and Harold Bushen is climbing up the steps.

132. The Greek steamer **Cianmoulis Goumaris** ashore at Embelle Wood, 2 May 1940

The years of the First and Second World Wars took a terrible toll of vessels. Hundreds of steamers were sent to the bottom in the Western Approaches and the entrance to the Bristol Channel. Captain Hugh Shaw told of the occasion in 1940 when he was bound up the Channel out of Ireland in a wooden sailing ship and found himself sailing between two vast lakes of burning oil. Having no room to turn either way, he sailed on through an ever-decreasing gap in the roaring flames and just managed to make it through. Two tankers had been torpedoed and their cargoes set alight. Another tanker victim which was set on fire within sight of the Exmoor coast was the *Inverdargle* and many local boys can remember seeing the great pall of smoke rising high in the sky beyond Porlock. Most vessels sailed in convoy but inevitably there were stragglers and this one piled into boulders at the bottom of Embelle Wood. The crew scrambled ashore and set up a makeshift camp on the beach before tugs arrived and managed to get her off. It was forbidden to take photographs during the war but this was taken and survived in the lifeboat house at Minehead for decades afterwards.

fig. 131

fig. 132

133. The Mary Stewart *in Minehead harbour, 1958*

By the end of the fifties Minehead had lost her last sailing vessel and the harbour had passed out of the hands of the Luttrell family into the ownership of the Minehead Urban District Council. The only vessel to visit Minehead that looked anything like a sailing ship was the *Mary Stewart* who made up in some way for the loss of the *Emma Louise*. Once a fully rigged tops'l schooner she suffered reduction to a ketch and the the further indignity of being cut down to an auxilliary motor vessel shorn of her bowsprit and jib-boom, her topmast and tops'l leaving only a gaff mains'l and mizzen to aid her

fig. 133

motor when necessary or to take advantage of a stiff breeze and allow the engine to rest. In 1958 she was bringing coal for the gasworks as the *Emma Louise* had done. She was launched at Montrose as a tops'l schooner of 77 tons and was registered at Greenock. With a length of 72 feet and a beam of 20 feet she was almost the same size as the *Perriton* built at Minehead seventy years before. When she was running into Minehead she was under contract to Rawle Gammon and Baker who continued to run her for a number of years. She was finally sold to American interests and it is believed that she sailed there to start a new life as a yacht.

134. The Promenade, 1960

This photograph was commissioned by the *Evening Post*, Bristol for a series depicting West Country towns and villages for their country editions and was published in 1960. This picture shows the ultimate development of the Avenue which runs diagonally across the picture from right to left. Marked with a cross is a tree which can be found in photographs taken of the town a century before. When photography was in its infancy a stream flowed unhindered down this roadway and emptied into the sea just to the left of the tree. The area with the trees and bushes marks where the original weir harbour

opened into its first basin before continuing along behind the sea wall to the right of the picture. The Metropole Hotel and the Esplanade building are set back at an angle because their foundations are built on the first solid ground to rise at the back of the old weir basin. Bores made in the early 1960s confirm this. The reader may like to compare this photograph with those in this collection taken a hundred years before and marvel at the extent of development.

135. Quay Street, Minehead, 1960

Also commissioned by the *Evening Post* in 1960 this picture shows the long ribbon-like pattern of Quay Street leading down to the harbour. In the right of the picture we can see the gasworks, the lifeboathouse, T.K.'s coal cellar (later to be turned into apartments), the Pier Hotel (later to be called The Ship Aground) and sailing boats in the harbour. Moving left along Quay Street you can clearly see where the road widens, indicating the site of the cottages that once backed onto the sea. Continuing left along Quay Street one reaches the junction with Blenheim Road, the site of Lamb Cottage, and a little bit further on the sea wall makes a turn to follow the present Promenade. Just by the turn is the site of the haven beach where the original weir was bridged.

fig. 134

fig. 135

136. Minehead harbour circa 1965

This photograph, a bird's-eye view of Minehead harbour, was kindly provided by Aerofilms of London.

With this photograph we may observe that beyond the harbour can still be seen the remains of Ossy Point and Greenaleigh Point were smuggling took place in years gone by. Much of the hill is now covered in trees and shrubs and the old navigation point directly above the harbour known as Compass is now shrouded with pine trees. The harbour sleeps, no longer a centre of commerce, just a place in which boating is enjoyed and visitors come to sit in the sunshine.

fig. 136

137. Dunster Hawn, 1947

This aerial photograph, taken by a reconnaissance spitfire in 1947, clearly shows the outline of the old weir harbour at Dunster.

138. Blue Anchor, 1865

This is possibly the earliest photograph of the place now known as Blue Anchor. It was taken by Date of Watchet and included in his famous album of local views photographed

fig. 137

fig. 138

between 1856 and 1867. It shows what the foreshore and shingle ridge looked like before the sea wall was constructed at the beginning of the twentieth century. At this time the hamlet consisted of a popular inn, a few cottages and a brick kiln that were built at the eastern end of the beach on the first high ground after the marshy water meadows that extended right across the bay towards Carhampton parish. It is probable that these buildings marked the beginning of the pathway that led along the cliff top to the ancient chapel of St Mary le Cliff which fell into the sea during the reign of Richard the Second. From this point westwards there were no other significant buildings apart from the farm building now known as The Smugglers and Marshwood Farm, a once considerable manor house owned by the Luttrell family of Dunster. It was a wild and lonely spot and the track that crossed the bay on the shingle ridge was often washed away in spite of being upgraded to turnpike status soon after 1765. It is not suprising to learn that this beach was much in use by the smuggling fraternity as it was well out of sight of both Minehead and Watchet harbours where the riding officers were stationed. The beach itself is subject to very heavy seas and countless attempts have been made to erect satisfactory sea defences. On Ker Moor, a huge system of pilings was built in the 1880s in an attempt to break the force of the waves and stop the flooding of the fields to the west of the landing at Bradley Gate but to no avail. They were rebuilt again in the early years of the twentieth century but there is very little left today and the huge iron bolts that once secured them can be found encrusted with beach stones and lying all over the bay. After timber, concrete and bitumen was used but they too have suffered over time. The present sea wall has lasted remarkably well although the protection of the seaward side has needed constant replacing and upgrading.

It was just here on the beach in the centre of the photograph that the Watchet ketch *Charlotte* was blown ashore during a sudden severe easterly blizzard in April 1916. She had been loaded with coal for Watchet out of Lydney and being early for the tide had decided to make for the anchorage off Grey Rock Point below the Blue Anchor Inn. The sleet squall that hit her had been particularly severe and the ketch was blown ashore in high seas. Captain Norman and the crew decided not to abandon ship as the surf was too dangerous to cope with and so they stayed on board, lashing themselves to the shrouds and enduring the waves that broke right over the stranded vessel. When the tide finally withdrew, the battered crew left her with the anchor out and started the long walk back to Watchet across Cleeve Hill. She was refloated the following day and appeared to have suffered only minimal damage. The *Charlotte* remained at Watchet until 1927 when she was broken up under the West Pier and, as was often the case, the bits put to good purpose around the town.

139. Blue Anchor, 1937

This photograph of Blue Anchor shows one of the attempts to prevent the collapse of the lias cliffs by erecting a reinforced concrete sea wall. No sea defences are very effective here as the cliffs are cutting back rapidly and on a still day you can hear the pitter-patter as friable material tumbles down onto the shingle. A few hundred yards to the eastward, Grey Rock Point or Blue Anchor Head has been collapsing regularly into the sea leaving massive alabaster-streaked boulders for the sea to break down which it does with amazing effectiveness. The alabaster is found in veins running through blue lias which is highly soluble and easily fractured. Alabaster was quarried here from

fig. 139

the fifteenth century and used principally for the construction of tomb slabs. Evidence that the cliffs once extended much further out to sea than they do now is found in the marine plain that extends from beneath the cliffs and the many rocky ridges that have yet to be levelled.

The old name for Blue Anchor was Bradley Gate and there are many references to Minehead vessels coming to Bradley Gate to load shingle, usually for use as infill. The occasional cargo of coal was delivered there for transport inland. The name Blue Anchor derived from the bay itself where vessels anchoring found their anchors covered with blue clay. The traditional point for anchoring vessels was off the Blue Anchor Inn. When the railway pushed on from Watchet to Minehead in 1874, a station was made here and named Blue Anchor after the bay rather than after the settlement.

Early in 1881 a tremendous gale struck the Bristol Channel area. Arising suddenly on the evening of 18 January, it lasted throughout two days. The Somerset coast was the scene of several disastrous wrecks. One of them, a Norwegian barque named *American*, was anchored in Penarth Roads on the Tuesday when another vessel collided with her. She broke away from her moorings and was blown out into the Channel. Not having had time to prepare for the open sea, especially a rough sea, she rigged storm canvas and signalled for help. These signals were seen by the members of the crew of a tug, the

Empress of India, which came under the lee of the vessel and took a rope aboard.

For the moment they were safe, but it became increasingly apparent that they were drifting fast onto a lee shore. In fact they had drifted right across the Bristol Channel driven by winds of hurricane force and were in grave danger of running ashore on the Somerset coast. There seemed to be only one way out if lives were to be saved. The tug came alongside, and the crew of the larger vessel were taken aboard, one after another, until eleven were safely aboard the tug. In the confusion and flying spray, they did not miss the ship's carpenter who was not on deck at the time and before anyone had noticed that he was missing, the tow rope was cut and the stricken vessel was left to drift. Just about this time it started to snow quite heavily so that visibility was cut down to a few yards.

However when the carpenter came on deck, he soon realised his position and tried to save himself. Hearing the roar of the breakers thundering on the beach he tried to judge their distance but the noise of the gale prevented any accurate judgement. Knowing that he had very little time left he doubled aft and put as much starboard wheel on as he could, lashed it and made for the ship's smallest boat with the idea of launching it over the lee rails. As the vessel began to swing he managed to get the boat over the side and, scrambling down the burtons, he cut himself adrift.

Almost broadside on to the driving sea, the vessel rolled heavily as tons of water seethed across her decks. Already the hatch covers and much of her gear had been swept away and the sea had entered the cargo. She had been loaded with salt from Gloucester to Baltimore. Only a short time was to elapse before she was driven with terrific force against Bull Ridge, a prominent shingle ridge to the east of Warren Point. Severely damaged, she drew off with the ebb tide and sank. The tug, having lost contact with the larger vessel, put about and steamed into the gale, ariving next day at Cardiff.

Meanwhile, the carpenter, Tallac Oslem, was blown ashore half a mile to the east of his ship, his boat capsizing in the heavy breakers. Quite by chance he was close to the signal box at Blue Anchor station where he was spotted by the station master, Mr Crang, who went to his aid, pulling him exhausted and breathless out of the freezing sea. He stayed at Blue Anchor until the railway line was cleared of snow and was then sent to Minehead. From Minehead he was sent to Bristol where he stayed at the expense of the Norwegian consul. Later he was re-united with his crew who were delighted because they had given him up for dead. This is perhaps the only occasion a station master effected a rescue at sea whilst on duty. Of the *American*, there was no trace and although the area was searched, nothing was ever found.

In an old sailcloth covered book which came out of the *Orestes* entitled *Sailing Instructions, Bristol Channel, 1856* is this description of Blue Anchor from a sailor's point of view.

Blue Anchor Head lies four miles south eastward of Minehead harbour; between which the ground uncovers half a mile out, all rocky, excepting just to the westward of Blue Anchor Head, where there is a layer of mud, on which vessels have frequently been saved which were obliged to run on shore. To vessels lying in Blue Anchor Roads, this is a valuable recourse, when caught with a sudden shift of wind from the north-west; and, if deeply laden, they must either slip, or sink at their anchors, for the bottom is so tenacious (blue mud), that it with the greatest difficulty yields. The best anchorage in these roads is in four fathoms with Blue Anchor House (the nearest to the cliffs) south-east by south.

The Blue Anchor House is, of course, the inn which has been an inn for centuries and is a mite nearer the cliff edge than it was when those instructions were written. Inevitably, one day it will go over the edge just as the little nearby copse has done during the last thirty years and just as the famous chapel of St Mary le Cliff did hundreds of years ago. The story goes that when the shoreline was searched after the disaster and the rubble identified, an unmarked statue of The Virgin Mary was discovered intact and declared a miracle.

140. Hauling limestone with donkeys

In the 1930s the limekiln at the top of Cleeve Hill, Watchet was still in operation. It was most probably the last working limekiln in West Somerset and was supplied by a team of hard-working donkeys that laboured up the hill heavily laden with wooden panniers of stone.

fig. 140

WATCHET

WATCHET

141. Watchet harbour.

Taken in the early 1960s for the *Evening Post*, Bristol, this photograph not only shows Watchet harbour but most of the town as well.

It was said earlier that Watchet is extremely old. We know that the settlement was raided in the tenth century by that multinational army of seafaring raiders sometimes called Vikings and sometimes Danes. They came to Watchet for money because Watchet minted coins in those days and its reputation for doing so had spread to all corners of the kingdom. That they were successful is confirmed by the discovery of Watchet minted coins in Scandinavia. Yet it was not as a mint or as a coastal market for the exchange of goods that Watchet first came to fame. Watchet was, quite simply, an important Celtic site famed for its water like many other ancient sites in the West of England.

The nature of the earliest harbour is to be found inside the town on the landward side of the road bridge that crosses Market Street. Here, the river was tidal for some distance upstream offering the opportunity for quays and jetties on both sides of the stream. Before the bridge, the road from Blue Anchor forded the river here despite the fact that at high tides the road was flooded. Vessels of up to 30 and 40 tons could be brought into the town although as the size of vessels increased it became obvious that some form of harbour would have to be constructed off the beach and protected from the prevailing westerlies by a sea defence. That this had been done by the middle of the fifteenth century is evidenced by Watchet's operation of the common practice of appealing for parish help in extreme cases to the church authorities who would issue a directive to all the churches in the diocese to send aid. Bath and Wells issued such a directive in 1458 and Watchet's name was added to the list of places in need of immediate practical help. The harbour is specifically mentioned as having suffered damage by storms, so it is assumed that a cob quay similar to the one that was built at the entrance to Porlock's weir harbour was built in the early years of the fifteenth century. Early maps of the inner harbour, which presumably was kept in use for as long as practically possible, shows the stream widening out into a basin and the sites of several quays where vessels could make fast. Like Minehead's quay, Watchet's was sheltered from the

fig. 142

westerlies but vulnerable from any winds from an easterly direction and it was to be the north-easterly gales that did the most damage over the centuries. There are records of the port seeking help for storm damage on several occasions but notably in 1659 and 1661. In 1708 Sir William Wyndham rebuilt the entire harbour of local stone for the sum of £1000. By the early years of the eighteenth century a much repaired but relatively solid quay extended from the passageway in Market Street by the cot of the quay to the quay head in a gentle curve of some 500 feet. The rear, exposed to the west, was made up of huge boulders similar to the ones that protect Minehead's quay and the inner side was lined with regular baulks of elm. The profile of this harbour was far different to the outline of the harbour today for before 1843, when the Esplanade was planned, there were many more cottages lining the harbour side and some of these enjoyed their own jetties and slips. The building of the Esplanade and a new slip destroyed many of these old cottages and cleared away the private slipways in favour of a new one for joint use. The Esplanade wall created a new difficulty however as, in a stiff blow, it encouraged the waves to rebound into the harbour and meet the incoming tide thus causing a region of turbulent water that few vessels could ride out without damage.

142. Turner's Watchet of 1811

This engraving based on a sketch by J. M. W. Turner in 1811 shows the harbour arm of 1708 and the repair work carried out on the quay head in 1721. It also shows the storm pilings which were set in the beach in 1807 as an attempt to prevent damage from the easterly gales. They were never very effective and did not survive long. The nature of the beach underlying

the present Esplanade and east wharf, the traditional site for local shipbuilding is also indicated.

143. Vessels in the old harbour, Watchet circa 1856

This is probably the oldest photograph of vessels lying in Watchet harbour and was taken before work commenced on the enlargement of the port to accommodate the iron ore trade. In the picture are four smacks, a ketch and a schooner lying up in the 'cot of the quay' minus topmasts and spars. The ketch with painted ports in the right of the picture is an example of a conversion from smack to ketch. The smack alongside is about the same length, if not a little bit bigger and shows the type as designed. Following the dramatic enlargement of the harbour completed in 1863 the number of vessels increased and there are many more photographs to illustrate the developments over the years.

This description comes from that local sailor's bible, the *Sailing Instructions* of 1856.

Watchet Harbour lies one and a half miles eastward of Blue Anchor Head and has the same depth as Minehead; the pier is the same shape and whitewashed. Here is also a breakwater of piles but is open to north westerly gales, which cause a heavy swell, and combined with the hard ground, vessels frequently receive much damage. When vessels appear to be approaching, a light will be shown from the pier head; and if it be their intention to go in, they are to reply by dipping the light three times, which intimation is acknowledged the same way on shore. The approach is obstructed by a shelf of rock and beds of rolling stones, which dry out in a north easterly

fig. 143

direction half a mile at low water. The best passage is to the north west of these. Bring the pier to bear south before running for it; and the beacon perch at a cable's length without the pier, must be left on the port hand.

What really guaranteed the survival and enlargement of Watchet harbour was the prospect of handling all the iron ore coming from the Brendon Hill Iron Mines following the decision to go ahead with the idea. From the mid-1850s, there would be work enough for everyone engaged in seafaring out of Watchet if the estimates were as good as forecast.

144. Watchet harbour as completed in 1862

From the mid-1850s the maritime community of Watchet experienced a tremendous upsurge in its fortunes. With guaranteed cargoes, the quiet country quay turned into a busy port and by 1862, when the new harbour was completed, Watchet became a bustling, thriving, enterprising seaport crowded with vessels of every kind. Even before the harbour was completed, between four and five thousand tons of ore were being shipped out of the port for South Wales. Vessels that had been concerned in the limestone trade switched to handling ore. Smaller craft took part and ketches and smacks lay alongside the larger schooners and brigs to take on ore. From this time forward the fortunes of Watchet began to rise. In 1860 the vessels inward numbered 445 and outward 446, with a tonnage of 13,954 and a revenue of £387. The figures in 1861 were

524 inward and 520 outward, representing 19,818 tons and £530 in revenue. In 1862 there were shipments bringing the revenue to £688 involving a tonnage of 22,759. Vessels arriving numbered 557 and the departures were 553. Timber, flour and paper mills were active during these years, all exporting through the harbour. Figures for the import of coal rose steadily during these years, the demand coming from the mills and the mineral railway bringing the ore down from the Brendon Hills. In 1862, the railway linking Watchet to Taunton was opened providing a swift route inland for imported goods and encouraging visiting craft to load goods inwards instead of arriving in ballast for ore, timber or paper. The story of the Brendon Hill Iron Mines is nowhere better told than in Roger Sellick's account published under the title *The West Somerset Mineral Railway* by David and Charles in 1962. The story of Watchet harbour's development from a tiny quay to the present day is ably and interestingly told by Ben Norman in his charming book *Tales of Watchet Harbour* published by W. H. (Ben) Norman in 1985. Ben's knowledge and interest is unsurpassed and he has added many local tales and traditions from the heyday of this once active port.

The new harbour, designed by James Abernethy, retained the old curved stone quay and added a wooden breakwater from the seaward side extending nearly 400 feet and terminating with a cast iron lighthouse and signalling mast. The east pier, built of stone and wood, stretched out to double as a jetty and a sea defence from the easterlies of some 600 feet and the land, beach and shingle of the old boatbuilding site was back-

fig. 144

filled to meet a new wall that would create new quays and additional space for unloading and storing cargoes. Well away from the mineral jetty which ran out on the old curved stone quay, these new eastern quays promised valuable space for the other imports and exports from the harbour. However, in order not to have to pay for the enormous amount of infill required, the Harbour Commissioners hit on the bright idea of selling all the land between the new wharf wall and the railway to the railway company for a nominal sum. The railway company snapped this offer up and thereafter the Commissioners were strapped for space on the many occasions when they wished they had the latitude to expand port facilities along the eastern side of the harbour. Of course the West Somerset Railway Company made a charge for use of their land and their facilities. The railway always insisted that they were also in the business of handling cargo and an uneasy relationship did not go away until the railway link with Taunton was finally destroyed by Dr Beeching. Nevertheless, some access was left and the quays here were used predominantly by the Stoate family who owned substantial flour mills in the town. There is a record of a Thomas Stoate taking a lease on a flour mill in 1832. He later became the founder of the firm of Stoate and Sons Ltd of Bristol. The Watchet mill was extremely successful and in 1885 was rebuilt and had new machinery installed. In 1865, William Stoate owned the *Hawke*, the *Express*, the *Quiver* and the *Tartar*. The firm later acquired the *Electric* and the *Telegraph* from the highly-rated builders Westacott of Barnstaple.

145. Watchet from the slopes of Cleeve Hill, 1864

This early picture by James Date shows almost the whole town shortly after the new harbour was completed. It was taken from the small field that extended across the cliffs behind the cottages and villas at the western end of the town. Much of this ground has since vanished into the sea and many of the villas have lost much of their once extensive gardens.

146. Watchet harbour, circa 1872

This photograph and the following ones are by Bert Hole who probably took more pictures of Watchet than anyone else before the turn of the century. The picture clearly shows the extent of the ground that was infilled by the railway up to the eastern wharf wall. Sheltering under the lee of the breakwater are vessels arrived light and awaiting their turn at the mineral jetty and a laden schooner, probably with a cargo of ballast stone from Ireland as some vessels, after loading out with ore for Newport, picked up coal for Ireland before returning in ballast for the next cargo of ore. Nothing was wasted, for a lot of the ballast stone found its way into Watchet buildings as a cheap source of building material. By the time that this photograph was taken Watchet had setted down into an accepted prosperity and had established every industry that supported its maritime interests. There were ropewalks, ironworks,

fig. 145

foundries, sawmills and shipwrights, blockmakers, sailmakers and seamen aplenty. All the pictures from this era show a harbour full of shipping and evidence of a busy working community. One after another, craft move to the mineral jetty as the ore pours from the Brendon mines. As many as eleven vessels were able to leave the harbour loaded with iron ore in a good week. The scene was alive with vessels, busy steam engines, noise and clatter and it all meant prosperity for the once quiet port of Watchet.

A report in the *West Somerset Free Press* for the week ending 6 June 1867 gives the names of Watchet owned vessels trading from the harbour. Incoming was Captain Allen's *Mary Lauder* and Captain Norman's *Richard* with coal from Newport. Captain Bale arrived with stores from Newport in the *Gannet*. The *Shepherd* and the *Laurina* entered from Swansea, the *Ann* from Newport and the *Express* from Cardiff. Captain Webber sailed for Bristol in the *Tom*, whilst the *Lloyds* and the *Abeona* made for Cardiff. The *Tarter* and the *Quiver* loaded out across the Channel with general cargo, Captain Wedlake's vessel took on iron for Newport and the *Shepherd*, in from Swansea, left with culm for Bridgwater. As the decade drew to a close, many of the smaller smacks and ketches started to show signs of heavy usage many of them not being designed for the heavy work they were doing and a fresh batch of vessels were brought to Watchet including purpose built craft re-inforced to withstand countless cargoes of ironstone and much heavy handling. Some of the smacks were inevitably lengthened and converted to ketches, some of them locally and some of them in yards 'over the Bar'. For the first time in many years, there was hope in the town that good fortune was here to last and investments were made in vessels. There were jobs for all and the youngsters in the town learned their seamanship out of their home port assured of

fig. 146

fig. 147

progressing from seaman to mate and master in the shortest possible time.

147. A locomotive on the turntable, circa 1872

In this picture by Bert Hole taken about 1872, the Bristol and Exeter tank engine No. 74 is on the turntable preparing for the return trip to Taunton for Watchet, until 1874, was the end of the line. These magnificent broad gauge locomotives had their lives shortened by virtue of the change of gauge which slowly pressed westward. Number 74 was one of a batch of ten built for the Bristol and Exeter Railway Company by the Vulcan Foundry in 1867. She entered service in August that year and was a common sight on the Taunton to Watchet line. The Bristol and Exeter was taken over by the Great Western Railway in January 1876 after which this locomotive became G. W. R. No. 2047. The gauge was altered locally from Saturday to Monday, 28 to 30 October, 1882 by a vast army of navvies

after which these locomotives were moved westward surviving west of Exeter until the final conversion in 1892 when sadly they were scrapped.

148. Bristol and Exeter locomotive No. 63 against the backdrop of Watchet harbour

Number 63, another product of the Vulcan Foundry, is waiting to go on the turntable. The date of this photograph by Bert Hole is likely to be about 1874. There are three large schooners and the one port-side on to the camera is probably the *Mary Louisa* a French built vessel owned by Henry Watts and afterwards by John Nicholas.

There were some big schooners owned at Watchet during the seventies among which the *Star of the West* must have been a favourite as she was built at Watchet by George Escott Geen, a member of a prominent shipbuilding family from 'over the Bar'. Built in 1859, she was kept by Geen for a few years, a sure sign that he was pleased with her, before selling her on to a syndicate of local owners in 1863. In 1869 she was sold again to another local owner, this time an experienced seafarer, one Captain Tom Davis who later sold half the shares in the vessel to Richard Date.

149. The eastern breakwater and east wharf, circa 1875

In this picture, again by Bert Hole, the busy eastern side of the harbour can be seen. There are two steam cranes in view. The

fig. 148

fig. 149

one on the Breakwater was owned and operated by Thomas Griffiths who bought it in 1870. The other one, owned by Henry Hole was mounted on rails and used to handle the heavy baulks of timber that were brought to the railway land to the eastward of the harbour. Just ahead of the crane was a large sawpit where a lot of this timber was cut up before export or transportation by rail. This end of the harbour was used predominantly for general imports and exports well away

fig. 150

from the noise and dust of the mineral jetty. Just across the broad guage railway track several heavily laden wagons are delivering a cargo of bagged flour from Stoate's Mill which will go down a wooden shute into the hold of the waiting vessel.

150. Captain Thomas Chidgey's painting of the Kelso

This painting of the *Kelso* by local Watchet artist Thomas Chidgey (1855-1926) was done for William and John Besley who owned her and was painted when the artist was in his early twenties. *Kelso* was listed by the Harbour Commissioners at Watchet in 1867 and recorded in the minutes of the local mineral railway company in 1869. She was a two-masted tops'l schooner of 67 tons register, laid down by Douse of Prince Edward Island in 1866. Compared with her contemporaries along the coast she was an exceptionally good-looking vessel with the fine lines demanded by the North Atlantic trade. She had a graceful fiddle-bow in place of the straight up-and-down stem-piece and gammon-knee, commoner in small schooners of the period. Intended for the Newfoundland trade, she was spec-built at Souris by John Douse and, in common with other Island vessels, she was partly fitted out and sailed across the Atlantic with a minimum crew to be offered for sale in Channel and west coast ports. She was soon seen and admired by John and William Besley of Watchet who became her owners and remained so throughout her life. She proved herself an excellent sea boat and a fast sailor. After continuing in the Newfoundland trade until the mid 1870s, she started regular trips to Ireland out of the South Wales ports. Captain Joseph Pittaway, who had guided her across the North Atlantic many times, was now able take advantage of more frequent visits to his family.

The *Kelso* was entered in the port ledger at Watchet, as shown by references to her dues there on tonnage. However she was not a regular trader from the port as much of her life was spent running out of the larger Bristol Channel ports of Swansea and Cardiff, Bridgwater and Bristol, but she appears regularly in the Watchet port lists, revised by the Harbour Ratepayers for the Harbour Commissioners until her untimely end in 1883.

The *Kelso* was indeed a pretty craft. It was said that she was as 'lived in' below as the cosiest home. On deck she certainly bore signs of her master's enthusiasm in the old practice of painting the Union flag on the cabin top. Two of Captain Tom's paintings show this emblem clearly. It is perhaps sadly apt that this particular painting of Captain Chidgey's shows her short-ened down under a nasty sky. She is pictured taking a heavy sea over the starboard bow while a crew member peers anxiously from the for'ard companion way as she prepares to go about. It must have been in very similar circumstances that she was lost with all hands in the Bristol Channel on Friday, 26 January 1883.

Returning in ballast from Ireland for Newport with Captain Willian Webber of Watchet as master she was making good progress up the Channel in a stiff westerly breeze. By mid morning she had passed Aberthaw and had the Holmes in view. Then the weather deteriorated and Captain Webber decided to make for Penarth Roads and lie up until the weather cleared. Many vessels were overdue that week-end owing to the south-westerly gale which the local papers reported as 'raging from Friday through the week end'. Against an ebb tide a sou' wester can be the making of a very nasty sea in the Channel, especially across the Culvers. Sudden squalls can whip the shallow sea into a fearful frenzy. Sometime in the early afternoon the *Kelso* was struck by a particularly violent squall. She shipped a heavy sea over the stern. Reaching gale force, the gust blew out the lower tops'l and plunged the bowsprit deep into the whitening water. A wicked sea swept the decks of the schooner, clearing her boat and hatch cover over the side. The bowsprit and jib-boom were snapped off clean.

Captain Webber quickly ordered the vessel to be brought about head-to-wind and the mate to stand by to drop the anchor. That the anchor was dropped is certain, but whether the *Kelso* managed to complete the manoeuvre is doubtful, for she must have been struck again heavily. She sank by the bows, the weight of water holding them down so that all that could be seen was the vessel's stern above the waves.

Towards evening, the brig *Pioneer* commanded by Captain Fowler bound for Cardiff sighted the wreck and went along-side to investigate. Though the seas were still high he could make out the name *Kelso* and Bridgwater on the stern. He put a line aboard and attempted a tow but the cable parted. After searching the area and finding only the ship's boat and other wreckage he wisely anchored in Penarth Roads where he stayed until the Sunday. Lost in the *Kelso* were Captain William Webber, master, Robert Searle, mate, Albert Strickland, A. B., and James Bale, boy.

151. The seaward side of the eastern breakwater and slip road, 1865

The point from which this photograph was taken by Bert Hole no longer exists as the cliffs are cutting back at a steady rate. The slip road to the beach no longer exists either but there was quite a battle over its construction in the first place. Apparently, when the Eastern Wharf was connected up to the Eastern Breakwater on completion of the new harbour in 1862 all access to the beach was cut off except by using the town slip and waiting until the sea had receded past the harbour entrance. This impeded such concerns as the limekilns in Govier's Lane which now had to make the longer journey and lose valuable time if they were collecting stone from the beach to the eastward of Watchet harbour. The harbour also lost the proximity of a shipwright's yard and a ropewalk which were swallowed up by the harbour development. Both had to relocate which they managed successfully but the limekilns were left with practical difficulties which limited their working capabilities. Consequently in 1863 a new slip was blasted out of the cliff face and remained in use until inevitably destroyed

fig. 151

by the sea. There were limekilns all along this coast and most of them had stopped working by the early years of the twentieth century but it was here at Watchet that the last one continued to function until the inter-war years still fed by manual labour and a team of donkeys.

This photograph also shows the mineral jetty, formed from the original arm of the harbour and now bearing rails and hydraulic tips to transport and ship the ore. Watchet was ever vulnerable to bad weather and within a year or two of the completion of the new harbour there was some anxiety expressed over storm damage. You can see the massive piles of timber supporting the seaward side of the eastern breakwater

but even these were being plucked out regularly by the action of the sea. The attack on this section of coast is harsh and if the very cliffs are eroded with ease there is little chance for timber.

152. Vessels lying in Watchet harbour, 1875

A calm tide is slowly receding leaving half a dozen vessels aground on the mud. In the background can be seen the wooden shelters that were built over the hydraulic tips in 1873 and the wooden construction of the western breakwater that was so vulnerable. It is interesting on occasion to look at individual vessels and this time they are near enough to identify.

fig. 152

fig. 153

From left to right we have the *Ann,* the *Astra,* the *Tom,* the *Friends,* the *Gannet* and the *Thomas Aylan.*

The *Ann,* a ketch of 36 tons, was one of George Passmore's vessels. George also owned the schooner *Crystal Bell* and the brigantine *Malfilatre* which was built at Caen in 1859. The *Astra* was a beautiful schooner painted on several occasions by Captain Tom Chidgey. Her name was shortened locally to *Astra* from *Astraea* which nobody could spell or say. She was owned by Henry Organ of Saxon Villas who was very proud of her. Next in the line is the little sloop *Tom* built in Pembroke in 1832 and only 23 tons. She was owned at first by John Thorne and later by Henry Waters. The *Friends* is next and there were two vessels of that name regularly in the harbour. This is the *Friends* that was built here in Watchet in 1852 by George Geen and owned by the Hole family. The other *Friends* was the one we have met before in Minehead and Porlock harbours and owned by the Ridlers of Perriton. Last in line is the schooner *Thomas Aylan* owned by the Allen family. She was built in Polruan on the other side of the Fowey estuary in 1860 and was owned in Watchet up to the early 1890s when she is recorded as being in the ownership of Bill Allen.

153. A huddle of vessels in the harbour, circa 1879

It is very difficult to identify vessels at this range but the French built tops'l schooner *Crystal Bell* is lying at the near end of the row. Of 94 tons, she was owned at Watchet for a number of years by George Passmore.

Stories from Watchet live on. They include tales of masters threatened with guns in their cabins, crew found robbed and floating in docks and others robbed, beaten up and shipped aboard clippers not to see their home port again for months. It was sometimes the case that local seamen, although highly proficient and well respected in their home ports were far too trusting and less careful than they ought to be when in the larger ports. Captain Bob Chidgey was in London following up the sad loss of his ketch *Louisa* when she was in collision with a steamer off Gravesend. He later reported how someone had 'drew his detention' whilst robbing him of all his money and leaving him destitute. This particular episode was the final nail in the coffin of the Chidgey family fortunes for he was to lose his vessel and cargo as a result of that last voyage to London. The story is worth repeating as it shows how often the innocent can suffer at the hands of the unscrupulous.

Captain Bob, with his brother Tom as mate and another brother George as cook together with Harry Vickery and a Bristol man sailed for London in the *Louisa* with a cargo of oats. When off Gravesend in dense fog they were struck heavily by an unknown steamer causing much damage and forced to take a tow. They later discovered the culprit with evidence of damage and paint from the *Louisa* still on her side. However no collision was acknowledged and in their attempts to represent themselves at a subsequent enquiry, they lost the case. The cargo was also lost pending the result of the enquiry and Captain Bob was forced to sell everything in order to pay the costs. The *Louisa* was sold for £150 for use as a barge and Captain Bob returned to Watchet at the end of his career at sea. One cannot help thinking that if he had had more professional legal representation and was not regarded as a rural skipper owner with one vessel he might have come home better off or at least managed to sail the *Louisa* home again. To be robbed in the street as well was the last straw.

fig. 154

154. A large Scandinavian snow unloading sawn timber

Exports of English hardwoods were consistent in the nineteenth century. Watchet and Minehead exported oak bark and trunnels, or tree nails used in wooden shipbuilding. These were obtained from the scrub oak that grew wild along the coastal hills. All regions of Britain depended on imports from Canada, the United States, Scandinavia, Russia and the Baltic where there were vast forests waiting for the axe. Throughout the Victorian era, one could buy West Coast Yellow Pine, Nevada Pine, Redwood, Spruce and a dozen varieties of North European softwoods. They were cheap and readily available and used extensively in boat building, furniture making and general joinery.

Here a Scandinavian vessel is unloading sawn sections of pine onto a horse-drawn timber waggon and the tracks show that they are being taken up via the town slip. From Scandinavia also came wood chip and wood pulp destined for the local paper mills. A paper mill had been opened as early as 1750, probably by William Wood who died in 1802. By the 1860s the mill was owned by John Wansborough, William Peach and James Date who had taken over from the Wood family in 1846. Not only wood chippings entered the port for the mill but cargoes of rags from home and continental ports. Local comments were often strong about the unwholesome nature of some of these bundles, especially in hot weather!

155. A Dutch schooner takes the strand

This photograph is a 'detail' from a larger one taken by Date in the mid 1860s. Here, probably loaded with wheat from northern Europe, is a typical Dutchman with her rudder 'out of doors' and having the prominently painted cabin windows fitted just below the deck aft. She is a beamy vessel with a pronounced sheer and stands out from the more traditionally built British smacks like the *Pioneer* alongside her on the harbour beach. She would unload over the side and the bagged cargo would be taken up the town slip to Stoate's Mill for milling before re-exporting via the harbour for Bristol or Swansea.

Most of the buildings on the Promenade in the background still exist.

156. The harbour in the early 1880s

The tide has just gone out leaving miles of foreshore uncovered for the work of the fishermen and longshoremen. Like Minehead and Lynmouth, the foreshore at Watchet was fished for over a thousand years and evidence of weirs, pools and gullies can be found extending towards Blue Anchor to the west and Doniford to the east. Like Minehead there are any number of old beach marks and beach names no longer to be found on maps or documents but created to delineate old fishing territories and local foreshore boundaries. Off Watchet harbour to the north east of the area known as the Fishing

fig. 155

fig. 156

Ground was Skobart Ridge and the western extremity of that area was known as Pennymar. Running on down to Blue Anchor were Smenny Flats, Cleeve Lines, Marshall Bank and Deadman's. Local knowledge was important as navigation by chart was virtually unknown in the days of the trading and fishing smack and all local coastal navigation was undertaken by reference to beach and land marks which were diligently learned. Unlike Minehead, which used larger fishing boats mainly engaged in the herring fishing industry, Watchet developed a particular style of craft shared only with nearby Bridgwater where they were built at the river port of Combwich as well as in the town. Consequently Bridgwater Bay and Watchet in particular were the only places to employ these unique craft which were unlike any other type developed around the coasts of the British Isles. There are many theories as to their origin but they probably developed from the Grand Banks fishing dories shipped on board the transatlantic schooners out of French ports. There were strong links in Watchet with Nova Scotia and it is not likely to be a coincidence that the local Besley brothers who bought the schooner *Kelso* from Prince Edward Island in 1867 were to be found using these dory-like craft for their fishing. Unless it can be proved that the design predates the Grand Banks cod fishing bonanza and the practice of dropping dories from schooners then this is the origin of the Watchet 'flattie'. They were about 19 feet long with a beam of 5 feet 6 inches and flat bottomed. Some were fitted with a drop-keel and a sprits'l but most relied on a deep rudder like the north-east-coast coble and were pulled. All had pointed bows and sterns which together with a good sheer was efficient at running up a shallow beach with a following sea without shipping masses of water. It was a matter of lifting the rudder and running in. The very shallow draught then allowed the fisherman to step out of the boat and make it fast. It also allowed the fisherman to service his stake nets in very shallow water.

Whereas Minehead and Porlock were using 30 foot open boats for drift-net fishing, here in Watchet both drifting and long-lining were undertaken by these flatties but in later years it was stake net fishing that predominated and the Besley brothers that had the lion's share. Old photographs rarely show evidence of these flatties in the harbour because they were usually moored outside the harbour and along the coast. The fount of information about local fishing was jealously guarded by John Besley, the last of the local fishermen. He was always cognizant of his father's words to him as a child that 'you don't hand folks your bread and butter!' and was zealous to keep all the family secrets about the best places to go for regular supplies of fish and shellfish.

157. Watchet harbour in the early 1880s

During the boom years of Watchet's trade, skilled seamen were much in demand and the local lads were able to gain sufficient experience to gain rapid promotion from A.B. to mate and then master of coastal craft. However the years of plenty were followed by years of decline. The mines died. In the January of 1883, 2351 tons of iron ore were exported through the harbour and in October only 134 tons were shipped. When you compare this with the October of 1877 when 4040 tons were exported, the difference is quite staggering. In the

fig. 157

harbour ledgers for the early 1880s, the final and lowest figure is recorded for September 1884 at 6 tons which must have been a part cargo. Yet the port did not come to an immediate halt. No port that had built up such a busy trade and had the resources in both vessels and seamen and the facilities that Watchet possessed could perish overnight, but the direction of commerce gradually changed and the port lost many of its seamen to service in deep sea vessels out of Cardiff and Bristol. Local vessel owners reappraised voyage patterns and ventured into the Irish trade and the continental trade, often leaving Watchet for months on end and seldom having the opportunity to return with any cargo for their home port.

fig. 158

158. An early excursion on the Earl of Dunraven circa 1867

Steam paddle-boat trips to South Wales and other Bristol Channel destinations were organised from shortly after the invention of steam marine propulsion and when there was little or no regular passenger transport available except passage in the weekly packet boats or ad hoc arrangements made with local skippers for voyages in sail. Even before 1850, Richard Date of Watchet hit on the idea of hiring steam tugs from Cardiff and Bristol for regular summer trips in the Bristol Channel. This was long before Campbells had even thought of coming south. These trips were advertised in the *West Somerset Free Press* and by handbill locally attract-

ing large crowds to sample a day at sea. On specific holiday dates, a brass band was hired to play on board and beer was available for those who wished to mix pleasure with pleasure. Not all these trips ended happily and on one occasion in 1850 six folk were drowned by falling overboard at Watchet. There was no enquiry and we can only presume that the unfortunate passengers had taken too much beer on board. The descriptions of these working tugs were set out in the most flowery terms and made these common little working vessels sound like luxury cruisers. In the 1860s there were trips advertised in the *Earl of Dunraven*, the *Neath Abbey*, the *Stevenson* and the *Defiance*. Date also organised trips in sail and there are recorded trips in the locally owned schooner *Heather Bell*. Crossing to Wales for the day was

fig. 159

fig. 160

common as was collecting passengers from Wales and bringing them to Watchet and Minehead.

Date was among the pioneers of organised excursions in the Bristol Channel and was not deterred by inclement weather, gales or the odd drowning. Every now and again reports would find their way into the local press telling of the shocking conditions experienced by passengers on this or that steamer but the vast majority enjoyed the experience and were very keen to repeat it.

159. The Astra shortening down, by Thomas Chidgey, Watchet Museum

This is the painting that John Besley admired so much. He asked the Chidgey family if he could have it and was loaned it for as long as he wanted. It hung just inside his house in the hallway for the rest of his life and only on his passing was it offered back to the family who were pleased to offer it again to other admirers of Captain Tom's work. Paintings by Captain Tom seemed to be in every village and township of the region, in cottages, hotels, pubs, terraced houses and tea rooms. One of the best collections was in the ownership of Bernard Perkins of the Ship Inn at Porlock Weir. When Bernard finished at the Ship he took his collection to the Rest and be Thankful at Wheddon Cross and following his eventual retirement, to his home at Carhampton. Bernard had pictures of the *Perriton*, the *Flying Foam*, the *Bertie*, and the *Florence Muspratt*.

fig. 161

fig. 162

160. Captain Thomas Chidgey and the crew of the Louise

This rare snap is still in the ownership of the Chidgey family and shows Captain Tom on board the *Louise* with the skipper, Captain Bob Chidgey and his other two sons. Captain Tom is second from left and, when this picture was taken, he had retired from active command and was content to travel as a passenger and to sketch, paint and draw during the trip. He couldn't resist giving orders or instructions to his son Robert but for most of the time he was happy just to be there and to enjoy his retirement. Captain Bob, second from right, was a splendid seaman and usually managed to avoid criticism although he was always aware that his father was aboard.

161. Herbert Henry Hole (Bert), photographer 1888

This is one of the occasions when Bert Hole posed for a shot himself. He is wearing the white coat he usually donned for his role of photographer about the town. Posing with him are vessel owners, hobblers and retired skippers clustered about one of Watchet's hobbling boats which is pulled up on the slip. Photos of Bert are rare and this one, from his own collection is a beauty.

162. Watchet harbour in the early 1890s

Another very clear photograph from the camera of Bert Hole. It shows how the beach slipway of 1864 has disappeared and a wall built to partially enclose the top of it. The picture also shows the wooden breakwater built in 1887 as an extension to the western breakwater in an attempt to prevent the heavy swells that drove right into the harbour on tides backed by westerly winds. As this was the direction of the prevailing winds the number of occasions in which vessels suffered damage within the harbour was of sufficient concern to warrant this addition. It was stoutly built and survived the great gale of December 1900 but was dismantled when the new west pier was constructed. By this time steamers were regular visitors to the town and here we see the *Helen* of Glasgow discharging coal under the steam crane. Two ketches lie under the western breakwater and a tops'l schooner is secured alongside the old mineral jetty

163. A Victorian regatta

Popular for decades around the turn of the century and only suppressed by the advent of the First World War, the annual regatta was one of the highlights of the harbour year. This one, probably 1893 or 1894 was no exception and Bert Hole has captured the atmosphere well with the vessels bedecked with flags and the crowd of spectators lining the western breakwater to watch the cutter race. A stiff breeze is encouraging the four pilot cutters visible in shot to press on with all sails set and the two nearest to the harbour entrance are about as close to the wind as they can get. Pilot cutters from Pill, Barry, Cardiff and other Bristol Channel ports used to welcome a break from their duties and enter all the local port regattas and there was much rivalry demonstrated

fig. 163

between the crews not only at sea but in the pubs afterwards. Many of the Cardiff and Barry pilot cutter skippers were well known in Watchet and were often in the harbour especially when severe easterly gales had caused havoc among the vessels lying up in Penarth Roads. One particular skipper earned the admiration and respect due to few as he had saved more lives with his cutter than all the local lifeboats put together. He was Pilot John Morgan of the cutter *Cardiffian* a man who demonstrated uncanny powers to sense vessels and seamen in distress on more than one occasion. On one particularly dark and wintry night he had just brought his cutter back into Cardiff after a job and secured her at the quay when he had a premonition that all was not right with a colleague pilot. Following nothing more than instinct he put out to sea again and crossed over the Bristol Channel

into Porlock Bay where he discovered the Cardiff cutter *Elsie J* dismasted and in immediate danger of running ashore on Hurlstone Point. John Morgan, without hesitation, put his vessel between the stricken craft and the rocks and managed to get a line on board her. Within minutes he was towing her back towards Cardiff where they arrived the next morning. The skipper of the *Elsie J* could not understand how anyone could have known of his predicament.

Right under the camera is the *Express* whilst to the right of the picture is the barquentine *Albert Baltzer* of Caernarvon. Under the eastern wharf are the ketches *Ocean* and *Friends* and a couple of unidentified tops'l schooners. Just under the lighthouse are a number of pulling boats waiting for the next race. The whole picture, full of figures, is a lively memento of the day.

fig. 164

164. The eastern breakwater, circa 1896

Yet another classic from the Hole archive, this picture shows the Dublin registered brig *Emma Ernest* unloading onto a cart. Welsh built in 1876, she was a regular trader to Watchet. Two tops'l schooners lie at the eastern breakwater whilst another brig has just left the harbour. Although by this time the iron ore trade had decayed there was still a respectable trade out of the harbour and many vessels that had been engaged in the iron exports were looking for a living elsewhere and seeking cargoes from other ports. Apart from Stoate's Mill and the regular imports for the paper mill long contracts were a thing of the past and it was a case of every man for himself. A survey undertaken in June 1897 notes that there were 14 vessels left trading to or from the harbour. The *Coronella* was owned by Isaac, Albert and Stephen Allen, the *Josephine Marie* by William and George Besley, the *St Catherine* was owned by Walter Camp, the *Thomasine and Mary* and the *Friends* (official number 10918) by Llewellin Hole and the *Star of the West* by John Hunt. The *Lizzie* was owned by Alfred Nicholas, the *Mary Louisa* by John Nicholas and the *Mary Lauder* and the *Aurora* by Henry Norman. The *Friends* (official number 21552) was owned by John Thorne whilst the *Express*, *Electric* and the *Telegraph* belonged to the directors of Stoate's Mill, James and William Stoate who held shares in all three vessels.

165. The Watchet lifeboats (a) the Joseph Soames & (b) the John Linguard Ross

The station at Watchet was opened in 1875 with the 33 foot self-righting sailing and pulling boat the *Joseph Soames*. Like Minehead, low water launching required the use of a horse-drawn carriage which used to take the boat out into sufficient water to launch her. Later this carriage was drawn by a motor tractor. In the case of Watchet it needed eight horses to haul the heavy carriage down the slip and along the least muddy route through the harbour entrance and out across the fishing grounds to the launch site. Her most dramatic launch came three years later when she went to the aid of the trow *Rose* which was being blown ashore nearby in a violent gale. Under the guidance of coxwain Captain Harry Press, the boat was launched from the beach but not able to reach the *Rose* before she drove ashore to become a complete loss. The crew were taken off by the local coastguard. The *Joseph Soames* hove to and waited for sufficient water to allow her to make the harbour. She hadn't long to wait before she saw the smack *Olive Branch* flying a distress signal and within minutes of following the *Rose* to certain destruction. With difficulty and superb seamanship, the lifeboat managed to get alongside and take off the skipper and the two crew members. Sadly the smack drove on shore quite close to the fast disintegrating wreck of the *Rose*.

On another occasion in November 1899, the *W H G Kingston* failed to effect a rescue of two Minehead fishermen who had been blown up the Channel in a severe westerly blow. Totally exhausted and unable to make the harbour entrance they anchored within hailing distance of the breakwater and trusted that their shouts would bring assistance. Despite attempts to reach the fishing boat, the lifeboat was herself blown away up the Channel. After some consultation, it was decided to launch a second smaller boat and this was done under the coxwainship of Captain Escott. Just how he managed to reach the

fig. 165a

fishing boat is still a mystery but it undoubtedly saved the lives of George Wills and John Bryant who were at the point of death from hypothermia. Once ashore, and this too took a supreme effort by the boat's crew, both men needed speedy medical support which came mainly in the form of brandy, massage and a roaring fire. The crew of the smaller boat were given awards.

The lifeboat station at Watchet came under threat in 1900 when the decision was taken to open a station at Minehead following the *Forest Hall* incident in which Coxwain Jack Crowcombe supervised the hauling of the Lynmouth lifeboat up Countisbury Hill, across the moor and its subsequent launching at Porlock Weir in the January of 1899. A strong petition was sent in support of retaining the Watchet boat and the sensible decision made that boats were necessary all along the 'iron-bound' coast of Exmoor and none would be axed.

A new boat, the *John Linguard Ross*, arrived at Watchet in 1903 and Walter Hole was on hand to photograph the official launch by Lady Acland Hood on 3 August. The following year she was able to save the ketch *Annie Christian* and her crew, thus justifying stationing a boat at Watchet. The last boat to be stationed at Watchet was the *Sarah Pilkington* which was brought around from Stornaway in 1919.

In 1944, both the Lynmouth and Watchet boats were withdrawn as they were 'old-fashioned' pulling types. In the meantime, Minehead had received the very latest design of boat, well able to patrol the Channel off the Exmoor coast and cover all the ports that used to support a lifeboat.

166. A beach launch

Captain Chidgey was always fond of recording the lifeboat and there are several paintings of the Watchet boat being launched or returning from a rescue. This is a detail from a watercolour in the possession of Captain Chidgey's great-grand-daughter showing the boat being launched from the beach. The coxwain is directing operations like a conductor with a full orchestra of professionals. This watercolour is one of a pair of pictures depicting both the launch and return of the lifeboat painted in 1913 as a wedding gift for a couple that left Watchet following the loss of work due to the closing of the flour mill and the decline in seafaring.

167. The tops'l schooner **Trio** and a smack alongside the western breakwater, 1898

W. G. Hole was responsible for this shot of the tops'l schooner *Trio* secured close to the grid which was constructed in 1896 for the repair of vessels. This part of the harbour was traditionally used for repairs and vessels could always be seen in the 'cot of the quay' undergoing some form of restoration or repair.

The *Trio* was a graceful schooner with a white painted figurehead. She was built in Jersey in 1876 and designed for the Atlantic salt fish trade with a good sheer and a high bow. She came to Watchet first in 1895 belonging to the Escott family who owned several vessels in the harbour engaged in the coastal trade. However, probably due to the beating she had received on numerous Atlantic crossings,

she had a tendency to leak rather badly and in 1909 she was sold across the Bar where she was remasted as a ketch. Somehow, she never looked right as a ketch and always presented as a mongrel with her hull out of proportion to her rig. In 1919 she was sold on again to Captain Joe Warren of Bridgwater who fitted her with her first engine. She then ran on through the next two decades of chancy trading before meeting her end by slipping down the muddy bank of the River Parrett at Bridgwater after securing there. She fell over on her side and was soon filled by the swiftly rising tide. Despite attempts to right her, she opened up and began to split apart.

168. The western breakwater and mineral jetty in 1898

The tops'l schooner *Trio* is secured at the western breakwater in the extreme right of this picture and the ketch *Ocean* can be seen on the left. Although extensive commercial mining had ceased at this stage, there is a solitary truck belonging to the Ebbw Vale Company out on the mineral jetty and a smack tied up alongside which suggests that an occasional load left the harbour from time to time after the collapse of the early 1880s. Some paper evidence supports the theory that a trickle of ore left the harbour on occasion but only as part cargo and not as a regular export. The account book of the *Ocean* is preserved among the local records and makes an interesting contribution to local history. The *Ocean* was

registered at Bridgwater but built at Aberystwyth as a smack of 49 tons in 1835. She had already done many years' service

fig. 167

fig. 168

when she was, like many of her contemporaries, converted to ketch rig in the early 1890s.

169. The Great Gale of 28 and 29 December 1900

Although there have been many disasters recorded along this coast there was probably no greater local catastrophe than the freak conditions that developed off the port of Watchet during the night of 28 and 29 December 1900. Combined with an incoming tide, a full westerly gale peaked to hurricane force during the morning and breached the timber framed western breakwater allowing the full force of the storm to enter the harbour where 13 vessels were made fast. Recognising that they were in for a blow, the vessel owners and skippers had doubled up the previous evening and were reasonably confident that their craft could ride out any resulting swell that might enter the harbour. Shortly after first light the first

fig. 169

massive baulks of timber broke free and were swept into the harbour. Within an hour the whole centre section of the breakwater had disintegrated allowing the giant crests to ride right into the vessels that were sheltering under the lee of the wall. Three of them broke free and were swept across the harbour to smash into the craft secured at the eastern end of the harbour. Four intrepid volunteers managed to launch a boat and attempted to get a line aboard one of the rogue vessels but they quickly ran into difficulties and were themselves swept across the harbour and were in danger of being swamped before they managed to catch a heaving line thrown from the jetty and save themselves. Before long the backwash from these huge waves started to attack the fabric of the mineral jetty which was breached from both sides and started to collapse. Until the tide went down and folk were able to get into the harbour there was nothing that anyone could do and the terrible damage went on as the vessels pounded each other to matchwood and sank. When the water finally withdrew from the harbour only three of the 13 vessels remained afloat and they were in need of immediate attention. The ten that were destroyed were total losses and worth only what anyone would pay for firewood. The names of the survivors became legendary and for months afterwards folk would come down to the harbour not only to gasp at the damage to the harbour structure but to look with respect at the *Commodore*, the *Electric* and the *Forest Deer*.

170. Captain Vickery on board his vessel, 30 December, 1900

The figure of Captain Vickery can be seen here clambering over what was his fine schooner *Hematite*. He was heartbroken

and brought close to financial ruin. The wreck was auctioned and sold for £5. Ahead of the *Hematite* is the wreck of the *Standard* which although looking in better shape was another total loss and not worth the expense of repairs. The auction of all that was salvable or useful only raised £200, a tiny fraction of the cost of damage done. In March the Harbour Commissioners approached an engineer who was then engaged on the building of a sea wall at Blue Anchor and he agreed to come over and make a survey of the damage and give an estimate of what it would cost to replace the western breakwater. The Commissioners were shocked to hear that it would cost £15,000, a sum that was quite beyond the ability of the little town to find.

171. The first repairs in 1901

Despite appeals at national and local levels it was all too apparent that sufficient money to make good the damage and losses would not be forthcoming. In the end only a few hundred pounds was made available which left Watchet wondering how they could overcome the problem of sheltering the remaining fleet of vessels still engaged in local commerce with a wrecked harbour. However, someone had the brilliant idea of re-defining Watchet as an Urban District and thus, at a stroke, making the rates available for the necessary repairs. Once they had established themselves in this way it was easy to raise the money on the security of the rateable value of all the property within the new authority. At the same time, the Wyndham estate made the town a gift of two hundred elm trees with which to fill the gap in the breakwater as a temporary measure and thus give shelter to the vessels once again.

fig. 170

fig. 171

This photograph shows the temporary repairs *in situ* before the new western breakwater was built. It also shows the damage to the mineral jetty with hundreds of tons of stone spilling out of the breach thus preventing any craft from berthing alongside. Both these ketches are awkwardly moored on the remaining areas of beach as the traditional berths at the western end of the harbour are covered in rubble.

The new Watchet Urban District Council sat for the first time in April 1902 and within three months were in a position to ask an engineer for estimates to repair and rebuild the harbour. By October 1902, a tender had been accepted and the work, which would cost the town over £16,000, was started. The new harbour was to be much stronger and the Western Breakwater was replaced in stone and concrete instead of timber. The mineral jetty which comprised mainly the old original harbour arm was demolished and the eastern break-water and jetties strengthened and refaced.

Just as the new work was completed and the ship owners were congratulating themselves that they had a splendid new harbour at last, another tremendous gale hit the little port in 1903 seriously damaging the east wharf and washing out the infill that backed the wharf wall of 1862. The ketch *Electric* was at her usual berth under the wharf wall at the time and suffered terminal damage. She sank at her moorings under tons of rubble. The *Electric* was built by the famous firm of Westacott

of Barnstaple in 1871 and was owned by Stoates Mill who also owned her sister ship the *Telegraph*. The *Telegraph*, seemingly had a charmed life for, as in the Great Gale of 1900, she had sailed two days previously and was not at her usual berth astern of the *Electric*. The costs of repairing this latest setback added up to a further £6000 but by the summer of 1904 the whole of the eastern wharf and breakwater had been rebuilt, refixed and refaced and the harbour was better than at any stage in its long history.

172. The **Electric** *and the* **Telegraph**

This famous pair were both built by Westacott's Yard for Stoate's Mill. The *Telegraph* was built first as a smack of 41 tons in 1869 and she proved so successful that she was quickly followed by the *Electric* at 46 tons in 1871. They are seen here in their usual berth at the east wharf where they would load for Bristol. They were both converted to ketch rig in the early 1890s but kept their distinctive smack lines with their straight stems and massive bowsprits which were designed to compensate for the length of their booms when they were smacks. At over 60 feet each they were bigger than many schooner-rigged vessels of the day. They were both fast and they raced on many occasions proving their worth and pedigree. The *Telegraph* was the survivor of the pair, lasting up to 1927 when she was laid up at Appledore in poor condition.

fig. 172

fig. 173

fig. 174

173. The ketch Electric

Captain Thomas Chidgey's painting of the ketch *Electric*. He painted her several times as a smack before she was converted to ketch rig in the early nineties. This picture was painted about 1898 and passed into the ownership of Thomas Rawle of Minehead who was pilot at Watchet for a while.

174. The reopening of the iron ore mines, 1907

One person involved in the restoration of Watchet harbour in 1903 and 1904 was H. B. Smith who became interested in the proposition of reopening the once profitable Brendon Hill iron mines. Doubtless he had been listening to the stories told him by vessel owners and skippers of the 'golden era' that made many Watchet folk relatively well off. He formed a group which he called the Somerset Mineral Syndicate and with limited capital bravely investigated the possibility of using the mineral railway to bring the ore down to the harbour as before. There was a lot of interest in his idea but there were a number of very real obstacles to be overcome before it could get off the ground. One of these was the lack of a jetty from which to offload the ore into waiting vessels and the first few cargoes were tipped over the side of the Western Breakwater using makeshift derricks and rope tackles. This photograph shows the unloading of the first batch of trucks. The next stage of this enterprise was to construct a

wooden jetty to replace the old mineral jetty that had been cleared away during the restoration of the harbour a few years previously. This was done and the line to the mines restored to full working condition. Sadly, as before, the demand for ore which looked promising at the turn of the century, fell off and the overstretched Syndicate found itself in grave financial difficulties.

By 1910 it was plain to see that much more capital would be needed if the scheme was to justify itself. Mr Smith was no politician and did not see the clouds of war on the horizon as many did. If he had been able to keep going for another few years he would have found that all national efforts to provide iron and steel would be backed by goverment money. Without such prescience and despite a lot of local sympathy the idea folded and the jetty was sold for a fraction of the amount it had cost to build.

175. The paddle steamer Barry at Watchet 1907

The main rival of Campbell's steamers in the Bristol Channnel was the Barry Railway Company whose Red Funnel Fleet vessels plied the same routes for decades. Here the new steamer *Barry* is recorded making her maiden trip with passengers to Watchet in 1907. This shot also shows the west pier just before the construction of the wooden iron ore jetty which was to project into the harbour adjacent to the railway lines.

fig. 175

1ST TRIP TO WATCHET BY NEW STEAMBOAT "BARRY" JULY 21ST 1907.

fig. 176

fig. 177

176. Captain Thomas Chidgey

The last picture of Captain Tom sitting outside his house in Severn Terrace. He had retired as master shortly after the First World War and handed over command to his son Bob. His second son Tom became mate and with George Chidgey as cook and Harry Vickery as A. B., they often sailed with their father on board. He lived the latter part of his life in Severn Terrace where his initials are carved into the stonework of Number 8. In the smoke-filled front parlour local skippers used to gather together and swap the yarns of yesteryear. On warmer days when the sun was shining he liked nothing better than to sit at his easel in the little paddock at the bottom end of the terrace and paint in watercolours. His subject was almost always the harbour he loved and he gave the results away to his many friends in the town. He died, greatly missed and much loved in 1926 leaving behind him a legacy of countless pictures of the town and its vessels which are now to be found the world over.

177. Detail from Watchet Harbour 1913 by Thomas Chidgey

In the mind of anyone long associated with the town wind and Watchet seem to go together and this painting celebrates the idea with a wild sea, tossing vessels and folk leaning into the westerly gale that is whipping across the harbour. The picture is full of life and vigour and is typical of his many watercolours and drawings.

178. HMS Fox in Watchet Harbour

18 July 1920 saw the arrival of *H M S Fox* in Watchet harbour to be broken up. She was, by far, the biggest vessel ever to enter the harbour and it was only by virtue of an extremely high tide that she was eased into a berth at the western breakwater by tugs. The firm responsible for this was a Cardiff ship-breaking concern who arranged for the use of harbour facilities at £90 per annum plus another £20 per vessel broken. Watchet thought that they would have a share in the large number of small redundant sailing coasters currently being broken in many local harbours, but they were not prepared for this giant cruiser which would take years to dismantle. However several Watchet men were able to find employment with the firm and the Council decided that a bird in the harbour was worth two on the other side of the Channel and so they accepted a further vessel from the same firm when the work on the *Fox* was completed.

179. The Dova Rio at Watchet

Between 1923 and 1925 the steel three masted barque *Dova Rio* was dismantled alongside the western breakwater. She is pictured securing astern of the remains of the keel of the *Fox* which was to vanish in the next few months. The *Dova Rio* continued to provide employment for a number of local men but in 1925 the Cardiff firm ran into difficulties and did not renew their contract with Watchet. Consequently no more vessels were brought for breaking in the harbour.

fig. 178

fig. 179

fig. 180

fig. 181

Ever since the First War, the number of craft owned or trading from the harbour decreased and by 1925 only four sailing vessels remained. Prominent among these was the Llanelli-built tops'l schooner *Naiad,* easily the most beautiful craft in the harbour. Together with the ketches *Mizpah, Charlotte,* and *Express* they were the last sailing vessels owned here although there were several regular visitors that used the harbour to deliver coal.

180. Captain Tom Chidgey's picture of the Mizpah

The *Mizpah* was another of the craft that made up Watchet's final sailing fleet and one of the last to go. She was built as a schooner at Cowes in 1873. At just over 70 feet long she made a big ketch when converted in the early 1890s.

181. The London Inn, Watchet

Although no longer called The London Inn, this ancient hostelry was the traditional meeting place of skippers and vessel owners for centuries. Many a deal was struck in the saloon which overlooked the harbour and it was here that landlord Captain Henry Chidgey in 1863 settled the warfare that had existed for decades between the hobbling crews that serviced incoming vessels.

182. The Watchet schooner Naiad

The last Watchet schooner *Naiad* (photographed at Bridport in Dorset) in 1930. Courtesy of Books Afloat, Weymouth.

183. The inter-War years at Watchet

With the loss of the schooner *Naiad* on Hannafore Point, West Looe, in March 1931 the last of Watchet's sailing ships had gone and Watchet's maritime interests were vested in the regular steamers which brought wood pulp and esparto grass for the paper mills. In this picture the Swedish steamer *Gertrud* is unloading wood pulp at the eastern breakwater which, in 1935, had again been strengthened and the end section replaced in concrete. The *Gertrud* had been built in 1881 at Newcastle for Swedish owners and was registered at Gothenburg. She was a regular trader to the town and a typical example of a late Victorian steam ship of which thousands tramped the oceans of the world. Secured just under the eastern wharf you can see the funnel of the *Rushlight* which was owned in Watchet for over forty years. She was built at Greenock in 1902 and came to the harbour in 1910, having been bought by the paper mill. Captain W. Norman made over three thousand trips in her, bringing cargoes of coal dust from the Welsh ports and the Forest of Dean to feed the boilers at the mill. He was succeeded by Captain Jack Allen in 1947. The *Arran Monarch,* which was built in 1946 at Faversham, succeeded the *Rushlight*

fig. 182

fig. 183

149

which was scrapped in 1953. She remained in service until 1963 when oil-burning boilers were installed at the mill and she became redundant, being renamed *Coedmor*.

184. A steamer unloading esparto grass for the mill

185. The Esplanade, Watchet 1933

This photograph from British Railways was another of those wonderful pictures that were displayed in the compartments of railway carriages. It shows the Esplanade before the cinema was built and when the lifeboat house still housed a boat and had not been converted into a library. These were quiet days for Watchet much to the disgust of the dozens of retired seafarers who now had little to do unless they left to work out of Avonmouth. Some did just that and Watchet and Minehead men could be found on the tugs and vessels that used Avonmouth as a home port.

Trade into the harbour was never as dramatic as it was before the turn of the century. Now, imports of coal, esparto grass and wood pulp were the only significant cargoes to be seen leaving the harbour for the paper mill and without the mill the harbour would simply have been dealing with coal for the gas works and domestic consumption.

In the mid thirties, another massive gale hit the harbour. This again was a freak westerly that rose to hurricane proportions and hit the Western Pier so hard that it split open all down its length. More massive repairs for poor Watchet but they were put in hand and soon made good.

186. The early 1960s

In the late fifties and early sixties it was rare to see two visiting steamers in the harbour. Here are caught the *Marius Nielson* with a cargo of grass for the mill at the East Pier and the little continental coaster *Veron* at the East Wharf. By this time coal imports through the harbour had all but ceased except for the occasional load for domestic use. Even the wood pulp and esparto grass were getting rarer as pulp was getting to the mill by road from the larger ports. The era of bulk and container traffic was just around the corner and all of it would be sailing on past Watchet for Avonmouth. The argument that it was becoming increasingly uneconomic to load small consignments for small ports was not very comforting for Watchet. The harbour was often empty for months.

fig. 184

fig. 185

fig. 186

fig. 187

СУЛЕВ

187. Watchet harbour in 1970

By 1970 the picture had changed dramatically. By a strange quirk of fortune, Watchet had not been included in the National Dock Labour Scheme and was not subject to the regulations governing conditions and pay for dockers. Throughout the stormy period of unrest and negotiations, Watchet remained calm and was not affected by the dock strikes and labour disputes that plagued the larger national centres. Time and time again shippers were forced to turn their vessels about and seek other ways of unloading their cargoes and Watchet was a port that had no labour problems and would welcome vessels to berth with almost any cargo. At much the same time, British Rail closed the Minehead branch line making land available for disposal adjacent to the harbour. This was the same parcel of land that had caused so much trouble by limiting wharf space near the east wharf since Watchet sold the parcel to the railway as far back as 1861. Watchet was delighted to buy it back and open it up for dock development.

Several businessmen were attracted to the town and by 1967 Samuel Tutton and Sons of Avonmouth and Charles M. Willie (Shipping) Ltd of Cardiff had set up headquarters alongside the harbour and taken up leases on dockside space. After that it was 'all systems go' and the ships started to arrive and the revenue began to roll in.

By the early seventies it was rare not to see a crowd of ships in the harbour and vast piles of cargo awaiting transport by massive articulated lorries that would thunder through the little town *en route* for the new motorway link. In this picture

a Russian vessel is unloading timber straight onto the trailers whilst a large stack is accumulating on the land behind. In the distance a new warehouse is in the process of being erected. High speed diesel motor cranes assist the unloading.

Samuel Tutton and Sons, having amalgamated with the West Somerset Shipping Company to form the Bristol and West Shipping Company, began to dredge out the berths alongside the west pier in order to start receiving vessels themselves. This added considerably to the volume of harbour and road traffic. Whilst the harbour could cope, the roads could not and huge lorries often jammed up the town completely. However this situation was not to last for long for the newly formed company neglected to pay for their lease of the west pier and their storage options on the east wharf and soon ceased trading. Charles Willie however continued to trade from the east wharf and pier and planned sensible arrangements for transport and storage under their subsidiary company Watchet Marine Ltd.

188. The **Are Friesecke** *unloading timber*

Here a local gang of casual dockers are unloading a coaster that has brought sawn timber to the port. By the 1980s a lorry park had been built and all available harbour space developed for warehouses and offices. The harbour had become sensibly and economically managed with the least possible impact on the town. However the new pattern was not destined for permanence. It soon became economically and practically preferable to turn

fig. 188

fig. 189

back to the larger ports that had the handling facilities, the transport links and the berths that could operate at all stages of the tide. At the same time Portbury Dock had been built around Avonmouth and was capable of handling the largest ships in the world most of which were bulk cargo and container ships that needed 'high technology' computer management.

Watchet was no longer viable as a commercial port. At the time of writing the harbour's future still lies in the balance.

189. Watchet from the air, 1964

This view of Watchet from the air was taken for the *Evening Post* of Bristol during another period of inactivity when it was thought that Watchet's harbour was destined for eventual closure. Somehow, like a phoenix, Watchet always seems to rise up from apparent disaster and enter a fresh phase of its life. Let us hope that as the twentieth century closes, further opportunities will arise to support this historic port in a way that emphasises its lengthy and unique history.

CONCLUSION

Today the sailormen and the sailing vessels have long gone and it is only in Avonmouth and Portbury that one can observe the arrival and departure of the ships and seamen of the present. As vessels are no longer owned locally and it is no longer the case that sons follow their fathers to sea as they once did, it not surprising that the sea does not have the same social and cultural impact that it had when it was an important commercial contributor to daily life in the region.

However, this is still a fascinating coast with a vigorous and stimulating history. After a thousand years as a busy crossroads, the changing pattern of life today has conspired to change the function of these shores. It is through the medium of such institutions as the Exmoor National Park and the National Trust that the whole region is bound together, coast and country alike. Having said that, within the boundaries of the Park there still live isolated communities who have never looked upon themselves as anything else but distinct entities. With the possible exception of Watchet – which was still busy with vessels through the seventies and eighties as she strove to maintain her links with her bustling past and to play a part in the chancy drama of modern seaborn commerce – a major group, the local sailormen, professional seafarers and shipowners have gone and the ports of West Somerset sleep the sleep of the old yet still clutching the memories of the time when they possessed a unique identity and tradition. Within the next few years, however, all those folk who have contributed insular and particular attitudes, traditions and values from this region's past will have departed. The individual characteristics of the region will have passed and it will make little difference whether one hails from Washford or the Weir.

Very soon all that will be left are the pictures by Captain Thomas Chidgey and some faded photographs in which even the vessels' names will be forgotten. Yet it is these very photographs and pictures that enable us to bridge the years and to use this primary source of information to appreciate the quality of life on this coast a hundred years ago.

For me the vital period for collecting photographs of the ships and seamen of the Exmoor coast was the 1950s when there were still many of the characters in the photographs alive and the stories were still extant. Many of these folk also had their personal albums to add colour and detail. However it remains vital that any potential collector or historian who wishes to take up this fascinating hobby starts now for every day sees the destruction of more and more material and the verbal traditions become more diluted and lose their veracity.

Previously published material on Exmoor ports and shipping by John Gilman

An Ancient Industry

Somerset Countryman
Vol XX No 1 April 1960

A West Country Tops'l Schooner

Sea Breezes
Vol 35 No 208 April 1963

Gale Warning!

Sea Breezes
Vol 37 No 220 April 1964

Storm Warning!

Longitude (Sweden)
Vol 1 No 1 1966

Portrait of Watchet

Ships Monthly
Vol 2 No 10 October 1967

Schooner Ahoy!

Ships Monthly
Vol 3 No 4 April 1968

The End of a Long Story

Ships Monthly
Vol 3 No 6 June 1968

A Painted Ship

Sea Breezes
Vol 42 No 273 September 1968

The Mariner of Minehead

Somerset Life
Vol 11 No 7 February 1969

The Legend of Easonton

Somerset Life
Vol 11 No 8 May 1969

Who Were the Sailors?

East Coast Digest
Autumn 1973

Bristol Channel Trading Sloops

Mariners' Mirror
Vol 50 No 1 1964

Photographic Source Material
for the Study of Ports

*Exeter University Papers in
Economic History 1972*

Captain Chidgey and the Port of Watchet

Maritime History
Vol 4 No 1 1974

The Exmoor Fishing Industry

Exmoor Review
Vol 19 1978

Grateful thanks are recorded for permission to use material included in the above.

SUBSCRIBERS

Canon Ian Ainsworth-Smith, Milverton, Somerset

Noel Allen MBE, Minehead, Somerset

Andy Anderton, Bedford

Alastair Brian Atkin, Minehead, Somerset

Charles Atkins, Exeter, Devon

Annabel Bain, Kensington, London

Sylvia M. Baker, Exeter, Devon

Amanda Barton, Martinhoe, Devon

Stephen Benson, Heasley Mill, Devon

John B. Bentley, Taunton, Somerset

Victor Bonham-Carter, Milverton, Somerset

Mr and Mrs C. H. Bowden, Porlock, Somerset

Jeffrey Brooks, Alcombe, Minehead, Somerset

D. J. Broom, Kerswell, Cullompton, Devon

John F Brown, Weymouth, Dorset

Sally and Jim Brown, Saffron Walden, Essex

T. C. Bryant, Llwyngwril, Wales

K. J. Burrow, Bucks Cross, Bideford, Devon

Sir David Calcutt QC, Twitchen, Porlock, Somerset

Peter Camber, Barbrook, Lynton, Devon

Mr and Mrs K. W. Carter, Sampford Brett, Williton, Somerset

Stephanie Cattermole, Kenley, Surrey

Elaine and David Chant, Sutton Coldfield, West Midlands

E. G. Chanter, North Molton, Devon

Roger Chapple, Barnstaple, Devon

Mrs Pam Clark, Maidstone, Kent

Mr John R. G. Cobbett, Denmead, Hants.

B. G. Coe, Kettering, Northants

Angela M. Cook, Fair Cross, Washford, Somerset

Roger D. Coombes, Pawlett, Bridgwater, Somerset

Mr Peter N. Cornell, Cambridge

Mr Dennis Corner, Porlock, Somerset

Hilda M. Cornish, Watchet, Somerset

Mr and Mrs Richard Crabb, Exford, Somerset

Mr and Mrs D. J. Cross, Porlock, Somerset

Penelope A. Cullimore, Lynbridge, Lynton, Devon

Davidson Family, Lynmouth and Ilfracombe Harbours

Dawn, Watchet, Somerset

Rowland P. Dell, Wootton Courtenay, Somerset

Margaret I. Elliott, Brompton Regis, Dulverton, Somerset

Exmoor Society, Dulverton, Somerset

Brian G. Finch, Caterham, Surrey

Mrs J. Rosemary Fraser, Colyton, Devon

Ken and Betty Gee, Carhampton, Somerset

Caroline J. Giddens, Minehead, Somerset

Liz and Tom Gilmour, Peterborough, Cambs

A. C. Glover, Lynmouth, Devon

Margaret Gould, Dunster, Somerset

B. T. Halse, Timberscombe, Somerset

K. W. Hann, Montacute, Somerset

Ronald Hardman, Parracombe, Barnstaple, Devon

Yvonne and Philip Harland, Kings Langley, Herts.

Dr and Mrs R. Harrison, Bishops Lydeard, Taunton, Somerset

Mr Jonathan M. Hawes, Enfield, Middlesex

Malcolm John Heath, Bristol

Brian Hicks, Cookham, Berkshire

Mary and Eric Higham, Wigan, Lancashire

Richard S. Hobbs, formerly of Minehead, Somerset

John Hobbs, Tavistock, Devon

Tony Hobbs, Merriott, Somerset

Paul Hodder-Williams, Exford, Somerset

Ken and Pat Hole, Watchet, Somerset

Keith and Pat Hole, Brompton Ralph, Somerset

John A. Holley, Nether Stowey, Somerset

Michael J. Hopkins, Milverton, Taunton, Somerset

L. M. Hubbard, Bampton, Devon

Christopher P. Humphries, Launceston, Cornwall

Peggy Hunt, Minehead, Somerset

Mrs. C James, Minehead, Somerset

David James, Minehead, Somerset

Malcolm Johnson, Horsham, West Sussex

Barbara G. Jolliffe, Alicante, Spain

Mr Adrian J. Kamp, Lynton, Devon

Miss Lorraine J. Kamp, Melbourne, Australia

Mr Paul Kamp, Lytham St Annes, Lancashire

Mrs S. A. Knifton, Bexhill-On-Sea, Sussex

Brenda Knight, Sampford Brett, Taunton, Somerset

Michael Leat, Bristol

Cor. John Lefeaux R.N., Williton, Somerset

Dr Christopher Lerwill, Colchester, Essex

A. I. A. Lyle, Oare, Lynton, Devon

Kevin P. Lynch, Barnstaple, Devon

Carole P. Mackereth, Dulverton, Somerset

Dr J. C. Malin, Minehead, Somerset

Peter J. Mann, Ninfield, Sussex

Michael Martin, Minehead, Somerset

G. C. Merrifield, West Bagborough, Somerset

Barrie J. Miller, Lynton, Devon

Ernest Mold, Lynton, Devon

Madge Money, Bedford

Olive Moody, Minehead, Somerset

Mrs Wendy Moore, Colchester, Essex

Mrs R. Moore, Hildersham, Cambs.

Patricia Morgan, Lynton, Somerset

Alan A Munro, Sandhurst, Berkshire

Philip Myott, Willington, Derbyshire

David Myott, Sutton Elms, Broughton Astley, Leics

John Neville, Dulverton, Somerset

Ben Norman, Watchet, Somerset

Mr David F. Osmond, Lynmouth, Devon

Oxenham Family, Lynmouth, Devon

Bernard Palk, Minehead, Somerset

Vivian and Molly Perkins, Porlock, Somerset

Mr Noah Perkins, Porlock, Somerset

D. M. Persson, Enfield, Middlesex

Nigel and Sue Pike, Bilbrook, Somerset

Mr and Mrs John Pile, Ilkerton, Lynton, Devon

Mr Hugh Pollard, Porlock, Somerset

Keith J. Poole, Tamworth, New South Wales, Australia

Victor Charles Poppy, Carhampton, Somerset

Lt Cdr J. A. F. Pugsley R.N., Plympton-St-Maurice, Devon

George Derek Purvis, Porlock, Somerset

Mr and Mrs Giles Quarme, London SE11

Richard T. Ridler, Porlock Weir, Somerset

Dr C. E. Ridsdale, Lynton, Devon

Robin Roberson, Tittleshall, Norfolk

R. N. Robinson, Kenilworth, Warwickshire

Rock House Hotel, Lynmouth, Devon

Mr Eric Rowlands, Luccombe, Minehead, Somerset

Howard Shapland, Wootton Courtenay, Somerset

Mr C. P. Sharp OBE, Maulden, Bedfordshire

Richard Shaw, Derby

Roy Shopland, Westhill, Ottery St Mary, Devon

B. and J. M. Skudder, Doniford, Watchet, Somerset

Mrs South, Brendon, Nr Lynton, Devon

Mrs Christine E. Squire, Lynbridge, Lynton, Devon

Joe H. Squire, Barnstaple, Devon

Mr Peter Sutton, Hawkcombe, Porlock, Somerset

Miss C. Thacker, Farnham, Surrey

Mrs E. A. Thomas, Woodcombe, Minehead, Somerset

Mr Roy A. Thorne, Harringay, London N4

Keith, Joy and Zoe Towells, Watchet, Somerset

Nathan and Ginnette Towells, Watchet, Somerset

Trevor Townsend, Sampford Brett, Williton, Somerset

Des A. Tydd, Lynmouth, Devon

Michael W. Tyler, Morchard Bishop, Devon

John Usmar, Witheridge, Devon

John and Freddie Vickers, Brentford (formerly of Timberscombe)

David Wardrop, London SW6

Robert M. Watts, Watchet, Somerset

Alan D. Weaver, Kings Bromley, Staffordshire

H. R. White, Liddimore Farm, Watchet, Somerset

Sidney Whitehead, Sidmouth, Devon

Susan Wilkins, Minehead, Somerset

Heather and Mark Wilson, Crowcombe, Taunton, Somerset

The Revd Geoffrey Wrayford, Minehead, Somerset

Mr Ernest and Lady Sarah Wright, Stogursey, Bridgwater, Somerset